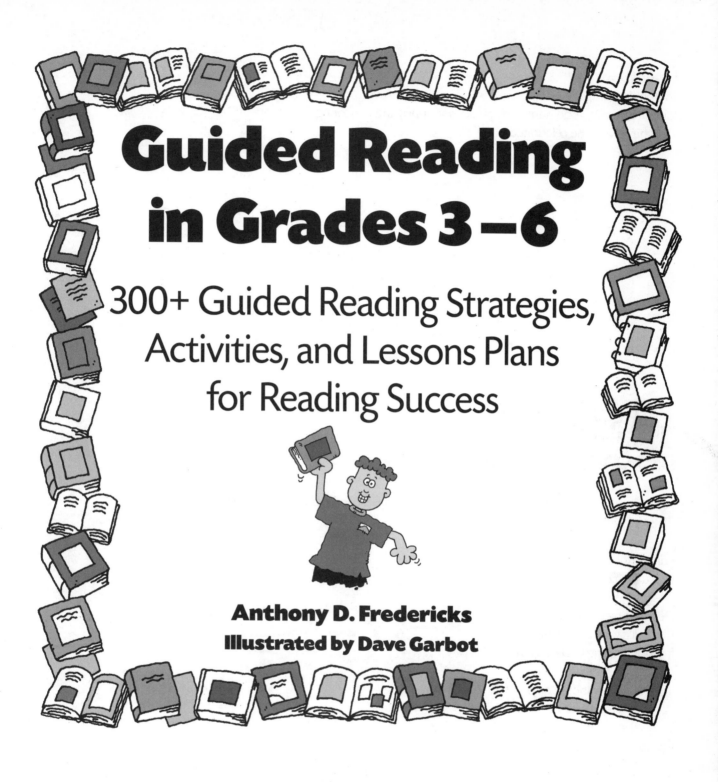

Guided Reading
in Grades 3–6

300+ Guided Reading Strategies,
Activities, and Lessons Plans
for Reading Success

Anthony D. Fredericks

Illustrated by Dave Garbot

Rigby Best Teachers Press

An imprint of Rigby

Dedication
To Bobbie Dempsey
for her constant good humor, continuous support, and endearing friendship—
may they always be celebrated!

For more information about other books from Rigby Best Teachers Press, please contact Rigby at 1-800-822-8661 or visit **www.rigby.com**.

Editor: Roberta Dempsey
Executive Editor: Laura Strom
Designer: Biner Design
Design Project Manager: Tom Sjoerdsma
Cover Illustrator: Bob Musheris
Interior Illustrator: Dave Garbot

06 05 04 03 02
10 9 8 7 6 5 4 3 2

Printed in the United States of America.

ISBN 0-7635-7750-2
Guided Reading in Grades 3–6

Preface

I WILL NEVER FORGET KAREN. She was one of those magical students who influence a teacher's life in a thousand different ways—a student we celebrate long after she or he leaves our classroom; long after a thousand other students have sat in the desks and etched their names in our memory banks; and long after a million lesson plans, a million field trips, and a million runny noses, skinned knees, and stubbed toes.

Karen came into our classroom one damp and washed-out October day. A pale and wrinkled hand-me-down dress, dirty blond hair, scuffed and stained shoes, and eyes filled with the stories of a dozen homes and a dozen schools, three stepfathers, unknown siblings, and countless hungry nights greeted us as we welcomed the newest member of our class. But, it was her first words that I shall always remember—words that are permanently carved into my mind as though I heard them yesterday. She stood inside the door, and with her eyes upon us all, she said, "My mama says I won't be here long, so I want you to learn me to read!"

And so that's what we did. Karen loved horses. We shared every known horse book we could find. We talked about horses, we created banks of "horse words," we developed Language Experience Activity (L.E.A.) stories about horses, we learned about famous horses throughout history, we studied the anatomy of horses, and we built papier-mâché models of horses. Every student in the class became Karen's mentor, helping with writing assignments, practicing with difficult vocabulary, buddy reading a new piece of literature, or selecting books at the town library. Projects in reading, science, social studies, and art all revolved around horses. Colleagues would often accuse me of spending my whole day "horsing around," and I would smile.

To this day, I'm not sure how it happened or when. But there came a time when Karen "got it"—when that imaginary lightbulb went on over her head and she understood. She could read an entire passage from the basal without assistance, she could engage in an active discussion with a classmate about horse racing, she could comprehend the main idea in a weathered edition of *Black Beauty*, and she could devour an entire book on her own during sustained silent reading (SSR).

Karen became a "regular" at the school library—often figuring out a way to leave the hotel room she and her mother called "home" a few minutes early every morning so she could spend some extra time with her friends, the horses. Karen often asked to stay late after school so that she could read the next chapter in a favorite book. She became a reader of the finest sort, filling her time with the joy and beauty of literature, as though the books she read represented the only time she would ever experience joy and beauty in her life.

Then one day in early February—a day when a thick layer of snow cloaked the school with a crusty patina—Karen left us. With that same pale dress and same scuffed shoes she, once again, stood near the classroom door. In one hand she clutched the fingers of the guidance counselor, and in the other hand she held a well-worn copy of *Misty of Chincoteague* I had recovered from my attic. She looked us over one last time and said, "Thank you all for teaching me." Then she turned and walked off to a distant school in a distant town in a distant state. In many ways, though, she was still with us.

> **T**he best teachers are those who *guide* rather than *lead; facilitate* rather than *assign;* and model rather than *tell.*

As an educator for more than 30 years, I have always tried to share the wonder and excitement of reading with my students. In my role as a classroom teacher and reading specialist, I worked to fill my room with literature and my students' lives with the skills and abilities to actively participate in, and become engaged by, that literature. It is students like Karen who have taught me my most important lessons about reading instruction; it is students like Karen who have most influenced my philosophy: that the best teachers are those who *guide* rather than *lead; facilitate* rather than *assign;* and *model* rather than *tell.* My experiences with Karen and hundreds of other students have taught me that the most successful teachers of reading are those who are able to provide students with the processes and the supportive arena in which they can begin to make their own discoveries and pursue their own self-initiated investigations. My students have also taught me that there is no one way to teach

Sample Schedule A
One 45-minute Block of Time for Reading Instruction
Groups

	A	B	C	D
9:15–9:30	Reading aloud			⟶
9:30–10:00	**Guided reading**			⟶

Note: None of the groups (A, B C, D) listed above is permanent. They are organized and arranged according to students' needs and abilities. Some may exist for a few days; others may exist for two to three weeks. The grouping paradigms illustrated above are not the traditional arrangement of "High," "Average," and "Low" reading groups. Rather, groups are formed and re-formed in a variety of patterns according to the dynamics of the reading program and the specific instructional needs of children.

Sample Schedule B
2 hours and 45 minutes for Reading Instruction

	Monday	**Tuesday**	**Wednesday**	**Thursday**	**Friday**
Reading aloud		15 minutes		15 minutes	
Shared book experience				15 minutes	
Guided reading	30 minutes		30 minutes		30 minutes
Individualized reading		15 minutes			
Paired reading			15 minutes		
Sustained silent reading	15 minutes				15 minutes
Language exploration		15 minutes			
Reading and writing				15 minutes	

The Foundations of Guided Reading

Many teachers subscribe to the notion that reading involves an active and energetic relationship between the reader and the text. That is, the reader-text relationship is reciprocal and involves the characteristics of the reader as well as the nature of the materials. This philosophy of reading, often referred to as a transactional approach to reading, is based on the seminal work of Louise Rosenblatt (1978) and has particular applications for teachers building effective student-based reading programs. As you might expect, it serves as a foundation for the construction, implementation, and effectiveness of balanced reading programs. Here are some principles of reading instruction (adapted from Rosenblatt, 1978) that will be particularly useful for classroom teachers seeking to implement effective guided reading practices:

1. Reading is a lived-through experience or event. The reader "evokes" the text, bringing a network of past experiences with the world, with language, and with other texts.

2. The meaning is neither in the reader nor in the text, but in the reciprocal transaction between the two.

3. There is no single correct reading of a literary text.

4. In any specific reading activity, given agreed-upon purposes and criteria, some readings or interpretations are more defensible than others.

In brief, this suggests that we all have our own unique backgrounds of experience that we bring to any reading material. As a result, we will all have our own unique and personal interpretation of that material, an interpretation that may or may not be similar to the interpretations of others reading the same text. Thus, reading a piece of literature opens up interpretive possibilities for youngsters and provides opportunities for extending that literature in personal and subjective ways.

Encouraging youngsters to become actively and meaningfully engaged with text demands a systematic approach to reading it available in the library for others to read before they pick up a Harry Potter book.

As you will note, this particular lesson deals solely with the first three chapters in the book. Marion knows that the concept of guided reading is a flexible one, allowing her to use it with complete books or with one book extended over a period of several days or a week. Marion has designed a six-day series of readings and attendant strategies/activities for *Harry Potter and the Sorcerer's Stone* that will engage her students in positive learning experiences within the guided reading program. She will also have multiple opportunities to use the book in other aspects of her overall reading program (such as sustained silent reading, reading aloud, and shared book experience), providing her students with a wide range of literacy experiences in a popular piece of literature.

■ ■ ■ ■ ■ ■ ■ ■ ■ ■

As you can see from these two examples, guided reading can be a positive and valuable aspect of any balanced reading program. Its strength lies in the fact that students are in mutually supportive groups—organized via ongoing assessment procedures—and are *guided* through authentic literature through a facilitative process that promotes independent reading strengths. The two teachers profiled above are examples of the thousands of elementary teachers who have been able to energize, invigorate, and stimulate students to become both active and lifelong readers by incorporating guided reading concepts into their overall reading curriculum.

References

Fountas, I. C., & Pinnell, G. S. (1996). *Guided reading: Good first teaching for all children.* Portsmouth, NH: Heinemann.

Haack, P. (1999). *Using guided reading to help your students become better readers* (Grades 3–6). Bellevue, WA: Bureau of Education and Research.

Routman, R. (1991). *Invitations: Changing as teachers and learners, K–12.* Portsmouth, NH: Heinemann.

Guided Reading Assessment

THE FOLLOWING ASSESSMENT INSTRUMENTS are designed to help you determine the appropriate level of reading materials in which to place individual students in your class. They are not designed as group or class tests, but rather as instruments that will assist you in selecting reading materials that are commensurate with the reading levels of individual students.

These assessment instruments can also assist you in developing appropriate groups. Your success in guided reading will depend on your grouping students who are relatively close in reading ability. These instruments will help ensure that process.

Administering an Oral Reading Passage

The Assessment is to be administered one child at a time. You may wish to utilize the services of room mothers, parent volunteers, instructional aides, or other adults in administering this instrument. The actual administration will take less than seven minutes per child and an entire class can be assessed in a few days (depending on your schedule of regular activities). The results will help you decide on the materials needed for a specific group as well as the students who can be grouped together for selected instructional activities.

Note: This is a simplified miscue analysis. It should be used as one element of an overall assessment process. To be effective, assessment must be continuous, systematic, and authentically integrated throughout the entire reading process. Assessment must also be multidisciplinary, using a variety of strategies, techniques, and procedures. The tools presented here can be effective elements in an overall reading assessment program.

To administer an oral reading passage, follow these steps:

1. Estimate the approximate reading level of each student using the following levels as guides:

3A and **3B** = low third-grade level   **5A** and **5B** = low fifth-grade level

3C and **3D** = high third-grade level   **5C** and **5D** = high fifth-grade level

4A and **4B** = low fourth-grade level   **6A** and **6B** = low sixth-grade level

4C and **4C** = high fourth-grade level   **6C** and **6D** = high sixth-grade level

2. Photocopy one or more of the following reading passages, making two copies of each passage, one for you and one for the student.

3. Present the student with a reading passage and invite her or him to read it aloud to you. (*Note:* Each passage has exactly 100 words.) Note each miscue the student makes by marking it on your copy of the passage. Use the marking system detailed in the table on the next page.

Marking an Oral Reading Passage

Example: "Black widow spiders can be found throughout the warmer parts of the world."

Omission: Draw a line through the omitted word.

"Black widow spiders can be found throughout the ~~warmer~~ parts of the world."

Insertion: Insert a ∧ and write inserted word above text.

"Black widow spiders can be found ∧ throughout the warmer parts of the world."
              and

Substitution: Draw a line through the original word and write the substituted word above it.

window
"Black ~~widow~~ spiders can be found throughout the warmer parts of the world."

Punctuation: Circle ignored punctuation and include added punctuation.

"Black widow spiders can be found throughout the warmer parts of
the world⊙" ?

Make note of the following, but do not count them as errors:

Self-correction: Write SC next to words that the child self-corrects.

spitters (SC)
"Black widow ~~spiders~~ can be found throughout the warmer parts of the world."

Repetition: Underline portions of the text that the child repeats.

"Black widow spiders <u>can be found</u> throughout the warmer parts of the world."

Adapted from Using Guided Reading to Help Your Students Become Better Readers (Grades 3–6) *by Pamela Haack (Bellevue, WA: Bureau of Education & Research, 1999). Used by permission of the author.*

Example Reading Passage

Name JoAnne Naylor   **Date** 10/8

Reading Level: 5A

Crocodiles are reptiles. Other ~~kinds~~ *kings* of reptiles include turtles, snakes, lizards, ~~and~~ alligators. Reptiles are cold-blooded animals. That means their body temperature is the same as the air around them. When it is *so* cold, they need to bask in the sun to warm themselves. ~~*what* (sc) When~~ it is hot, they must ~~retreat~~ *remain* to the shade to cool down. Unlike humans, reptiles don't have a constant body temperature.

Many people think *that* crocodiles and alligators are ~~very~~ similar. They often get them confused because they look so much alike. But ~~they are~~ *are they* really quite different? There are four ways to tell them apart.

Scoring:

Omissions:	2	Self-corrections:	1
Insertions:	2	Repetitions:	1
Substitutions:	3		
Punctuation:	1		
Total:	8	**Overall Score:** 100 – 8 =	92

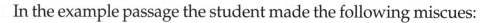

In the example passage the student made the following miscues:

1. Substituted *kings* for *kinds* (1 substitution error)

2. Omitted *and* (1 omission error)

3. Inserted *so* between *is* and *cold* (1 insertion error)

4. Repeated "to bask in the sun" (no error)

5. Substituted *What* for *When*, then self-corrected (no error)

6. Substituted *remain* for *retreat* (1 substitution error)

7. Inserted *that* between *think* and *crocodiles* (1 insertion error)

8. Omitted *very* (1 omission error)

9. Substituted "are they" for "they are" (1 substitution error)

10. Replaced a period with a question mark (1 punctuation error)

The student had 8 recorded errors. Since the passage was exactly 100 words long, the teacher subtracts the total number of recorded errors from 100. In this case, the final score is 92%.

Selecting a Text for Guided Reading

Too Easy: The text is too easy when there is almost no challenge for the reader.
Score: 95% or better

Just Right: The text is just right when the reader reads with some degree of comfort and needs some support.
Score: 90–95%

Too Difficult: The text is too difficult when the reader reads with difficulty and little comprehension.
Score: less than 90%

Based upon the score Jo Anne obtained on the Example Reading Passage—above (92%)—she would find reading material at the low fifth-grade level (5A) to be "Just Right." Jo Anne's teacher may wish to provide her with one or two additional passages at the low fifth-grade level. This will help verify the results obtained during this assessment.

Following are 16 passages, four for each grade from 3 to 6, to use in assessing your students' reading levels.

Reading Passages

Name _____   **Date** _____

Reading Level: 3A

The water was deep and cold, but I wasn't afraid.
I jumped in and swam for the sailboat. It seemed so far away.
I didn't know how it got untied, but I knew I had to retrieve it.
I could hear the waterfall in the distance and it made a
powerful sound.

I swam using slow, deliberate strokes. I didn't want to get
tired too soon. I have always been a good swimmer and a safe
one, too. For now, the boat was just drifting. I decided to take
my time and be very careful—I didn't need any surprises.

Scoring:

Omissions: _____   Self-corrections: _____
Insertions: _____   Repetitions: _____
Substitutions: _____
Punctuation: _____

Total: _____   **Overall Score:** 100 – _____ = ☐

Name _____ **Date** _____

Reading Level: 3B

    This morning my mother made me clean my room. She told me I had to pick up my clothes. She told me to take them to the basement and put them in the hamper. I don't understand why I need to have my clothes washed because I'll just get them dirty again. Then I'll have to take them to the basement and put them in the hamper again. My mother makes me pick up my toys and put them away. She knows I'll just take them out again and then I'll have to pick them up again. It's really strange.

Scoring:

Omissions: _____   Self-corrections: _____

Insertions: _____   Repetitions: _____

Substitutions: _____

Punctuation: _____

Total: _____   **Overall Score:** 100 – _____ = ☐

Name _____ **Date** _____

Reading Level: 4C

One look at Pecos Bill and you might think he was just an ordinary cowboy from Texas. Well, you'd be wrong, because if there was one thing that Bill wasn't—it was ordinary. And if there's one state that isn't ordinary, then it must be Texas.

Now Bill wasn't originally from Texas. In fact, he was born back east somewhere. He was the youngest of sixteen children. Being the smallest of all the kids, Bill always got the hand-me-downs of his brothers and sisters. He never got any clothes or toys of his own, that is, until he wrestled a grizzly bear.

Scoring:

Omissions: _____   Self-corrections: _____

Insertions: _____   Repetitions: _____

Substitutions: _____

Punctuation: _____

Total: _____   **Overall Score:** 100 – _____ = ☐

Name _____ **Date** _____

Reading Level: 4D

Doug's new computer arrived in the early morning. He removed all the packing material and gently took it out of the box. He made a space for it on his desk. With sure hands he made all the connections and turned on his new toy.

It was only a few seconds later when Doug saw something strange. He was surfing through some material on stars for a school report. On every page he noticed a small box appear in the upper left-hand corner of the screen. Inside the box was a gray-green ghost that moved slowly from side to side.

Scoring:

Omissions:	_____	Self-corrections:	_____
Insertions:	_____	Repetitions:	_____
Substitutions:	_____		
Punctuation:	_____		

Total: _____   **Overall Score:** 100 – _____ = ☐

Name _____   **Date** _____

Reading Level: 6A

Cowbirds live throughout North and South America. They do not build nests, but lay their oversized eggs in the nests of other birds and leave, never to return. Many times, the new parents don't notice the larger eggs in the nest. When the baby cowbirds hatch, they are often much bigger than any of the other birds. The baby cowbirds frequently push the much smaller babies out of the nest. The new parents don't notice the missing babies and spend all of their time feeding the oversized intruders. This may seem cruel, but it's how cowbirds are able to survive.

Scoring:

Omissions: _____   Self-corrections: _____
Insertions: _____   Repetitions: _____
Substitutions: _____
Punctuation: _____
Total: _____   **Overall Score:** 100 − _____ = ☐

Name _____ **Date** _____

Reading Level: 6B

The rhinoceros has been around for millions of years. There are five different kinds of rhinos—the Black Rhino, the White Rhino, the Javan Rhino, the Sumatran Rhino, and the Indian Rhino. The Indian Rhino has one horn; the other four all have two horns. The name rhinoceros actually means "nose horn."

Many people think rhino horns are very valuable. The rhinoceros is killed because of its horn. Horns are made into medicines that are believed to cure headaches and fevers. A single rhino horn may be priced as high as $5,000. As a result, rhinos are in great danger.

Scoring:

Omissions: _____   Self-corrections: _____

Insertions: _____   Repetitions: _____

Substitutions: _____

Punctuation: _____

Total: _____   **Overall Score:** 100 – _____ = ☐

Name _____ **Date** _____

Reading Level: 6C

Where do you live? Do you live in a city, a town, a hamlet, a borough, or a village? Each one of those places represents a group of people who live in a specific geographic area. On the other hand, you may live in a rural area—an area where there are few people or the houses are far apart from each other. One of the chief reasons why people live where they do is economics. That is, they may have jobs in a nearby city or they may have an occupation that requires lots of land—such as farmers.

Scoring:

Omissions: _____   Self-corrections: _____

Insertions: _____   Repetitions: _____

Substitutions: _____

Punctuation: _____

Total: _____   **Overall Score:** 100 – _____ = ☐

Name _____ **Date** _____

Reading Level: 6D

According to a Mayan legend, the first two hummingbirds were created from feather scraps. These scraps were left over after the construction of all the other birds. The god who made the hummingbirds was so pleased with these creations that he held an elaborate wedding ceremony for them. Butterflies marked out the edges and corners of a majestic room. Spiders spun intricate webs to make a bridal pathway. Flower petals formed a rich carpet upon the ground. The sun sent down rays of golden sunlight. According to the legend, the hummingbirds of today are the result of that first union.

Scoring:

Omissions: _____   Self-corrections: _____

Insertions: _____   Repetitions: _____

Substitutions: _____

Punctuation: _____

Total: _____   **Overall Score:** 100 – _____ = [ ]

Guided Reading Assessment Scoring Rubric

Directions: Administer an assessment story to a student. After scoring the reading, look at the chart above. Place a check mark in one of the three boxes following the grade level designation of the story (according to the percentage score the students obtained). You may wish to give the student a story that is one level above and another that is one level below the first story. That will help you pinpoint an approximate reading level for the student. The position of the check marks (such as Too Easy, Just Right, Too Difficult) will indicate the leveled books appropriate for that individual.

Name _____ Date _____

	Too Easy	**Just Right**	**Too Difficult**
Low Third (3A)	95–100%	90–95%	0–89%
Low Third (3B)	95–100%	90–95%	0–89%
High Third (3C)	95–100%	90–95%	0–89%
High Third (3D)	95–100%	90–95%	0–89%
Low Fourth (4A)	95–100%	90–95%	0–89%
Low Fourth (4B)	95–100%	90–95%	0–89%
High Fourth (4C)	95–100%	90–95%	0–89%
High Fourth (4D)	95–100%	90–95%	0–89%
Low Fifth (5A)	95–100%	90–95%	0–89%
Low Fifth (5B)	95–100%	90–95%	0–89%
High Fifth (5C)	95–100%	90–95%	0–89%
High Fifth (5D)	95–100%	90–95%	0–89%
Low Sixth (6A)	95–100%	90–95%	0–89%
Low Sixth (6B)	95–100%	90–95%	0–89%
High Sixth (6C)	95–100%	90–95%	0–89%
High Sixth (6D)	95–100%	90–95%	0–89%

Assessment Grid

Directions: Write the names of all of your students down the left side of this grid. Place a check mark in one of the boxes following each student's name to indicate her or his performance on the assessment stories. Upon completion, you will be able to note the students (at the same reading level) who can be placed together into a guided reading group. Note: Since you will want to do continuous assessment throughout the school year and throughout the reading program, you may find it advantageous to make multiple photocopies of this form (with students' names filled in) for use throughout the year.

Names	3A	3B	3C	3D	4A	4B	4C	4D	5A	5B	5C	5D	6A	6B	6C	6D

Comprehension Checks

The modified miscue analysis passages presented in the previous section are primarily designed to assist you in placing students in the proper level of reading material for a guided reading program. As shared earlier, they are but one element in an overall assessment program. Undoubtedly, you will discover that many students will be able to decode a passage beautifully but will be unable to comprehend what they read. In essence, a simple miscue does not (and is not intended to) reflect the comprehension of a passage.

As part of an overall reading assessment, you may wish to gauge individual student levels of comprehension. Following are comprehension questions for each of the stories presented in this chapter. These questions are based on Bloom's taxonomy (Bloom et al., 1956) and contain six levels arranged in hierarchical form, from the least complex to the most complex. The six levels are:

Knowledge

Questions at this level are used to determine whether students can recall or identify factual information in text.

Comprehension

These questions are those in which students must organize, assemble, or combine factual information into a grouping or cluster of ideas.

Application

At the application level students are asked to take information they already know and apply it to a new situation.

Analysis

At the analysis level students must be able to identify the elements making up the whole, see the relationships of the parts, and break down the whole into its related parts.

Synthesis

Synthesis is the ability to combine two or more facts into a new whole. It is the level that elicits and rewards creativity.

Evaluation

Evaluation requires an individual to make a judgement about something—that is, to make a personal statement about the value, worth, or rank of specific information.

After a student has completed the oral reading of a passage, you may wish to ask her or him the following questions. Ask all six questions for each passage. Note the student's responses and compare the number of correct responses with this chart:

Independent Level: The student can read the text independently with 95% or better comprehension. *Number of correct questions: 6.*

Instructional Level: The student can read the text with some instructional assistance and with 90–95% comprehension. *Number of correct questions: 5.*

Frustration Level: The student is frustrated by the text and has a comprehension level of 75% or below. *Number of correct questions: 0–4.*

Please keep in mind that this part of the assessment process is optional and does not have to be part of a guided reading program. However, this "quick and easy" comprehension assessment can yield some additional data in combination with oral reading abilities.

Story 3A
1. What was the narrator swimming toward? *(the boat)*
2. Describe how the swimmer was swimming. *(deliberate strokes, carefully, slow)*
3. What would happen if the swimmer swam fast? *(he or she might get tired)*
4. Why was the waterfall important? *(it might be dangerous)*
5. How else could the narrator have retrieved the boat? *(helicopter, long rope)*
6. Do you think the narrator did the right thing?

Story 3B
1. Where did the narrator put the clothes? *(in the hamper)*
2. What kinds of things did the narrator have to pick up? *(clothes, toys)*
3. What would happen if the clothes were left on the floor? *(mother would get angry)*
4. Where would the toys be placed? *(in a toy box)*

5. Why do the clothes have to be picked up? *(to be washed, neatness)*

6. How is the narrator like you?

Story 3C

1. Describe a toad. *(stout, dry and bumpy skin)*

2. What sometimes happens at ponds? *(toads find other toads and mate)*

3. What would happen if toads did not sing? *(couldn't find a mate)*

4. What are three things toads must do before mating? *(get to pond, sing, find mate)*

5. How else could toads identify members of their species? *(coloration, size)*

6. What else would you like to learn about toads?

Story 3D

1. Name some reptiles. *(turtles, crocodiles, alligators, snakes, lizards)*

2. What are some reptile characteristics? *(cold-blooded, related to dinosaurs)*

3. Why do turtles have shells? *(protection)*

4. Why don't turtles live in arctic regions? *(too cold, can't survive)*

5. What would you need to include in a turtle terrarium? *(heat, food, shade)*

6. What is the most amazing fact about turtles?

Story 4A

1. Where do giant squids live? *(the Atlantic Ocean)*

2. How big are giant squids *(sixty feet long, weigh one ton)*

3. Why are their eyes so big? *(to see in the dark depths of the ocean)*

4. What are the major differences between giant squids and regular squids? *(size, weight, length, habitat)*

5. Where are some places you might see a giant squid? *(no one has seen a live one; dead ones on the beach)*

6. Why would you want to see a live giant squid?

Story 4B

1. Where did this story take place? *(desert)*

2. Describe the sun. *(searing, hot, bright)*

3. What might happen to Caroline? *(become lost, die of thirst)*

4. Why was Caroline so frightened? *(lost, alone, hot)*

5. How could Caroline find her way? *(follow the sun, follow animals)*

6. How do you think this story will turn out?

Story 4C

1. Who is this story about? *(Pecos Bill)*

2. In what kind of family did the main character live? *(very large)*

3. Why would he wrestle a grizzly bear? *(to have a toy, to get some clothes)*

4. Why is Texas different from other states? *(big, not ordinary)*

5. How else could Bill have gotten some clothes? *(buy them, swap them)*

6. What type of story do you think this is going to be?

Story 4D

1. What was the character's name? *(Doug)*

2. What did he do with his new computer? *(unwrapped it, set it up, turned it on)*

3. What did the character have to do before turning on the computer? *(plug it in)*

4. What is the major difference between a computer and a television? *(computers are interactive)*

5. What could the character have done about the strange shape? *(turn off the computer, make screen adjustments, modify settings)*

6. What do you think the gray-green ghost signifies?

Story 5A

1. What's one of the world's most unusual insects? *(mayflies)*

2. What are some unusual features of a mayfly? *(can't eat, live for a day)*

3. What would happen if adult mayflies had mouthparts? *(would be able to eat, might live longer)*

4. Why do mayflies produce so many eggs? *(lots of offspring, ensures survival of species)*

5. Describe the stages of a mayfly's life. *(egg, baby, adult)*

6. Why do you think mayflies are so unusual?

Story 5B

1. Where did this story take place? (*Hazard Elementary School*)
2. What did everyone at the school do? *(was grumpy, mean, sad)*
3. How was Mr. Blithe going to change the school? *(by being happy all the time)*
4. What were some of the similarities between students and teachers? *(always upset, angry, mean)*
5. Why didn't anyone think Mr. Blithe would last long? *(he was new, he was different)*
6. Would you want to go to Hazard Elementary School?

Story 5C

1. What time of day did this story take place? *(in the morning)*
2. What were Brian and his grandfather going to do? *(go fishing)*
3. Why did Brian want to "cast his line"? *(keep it away from the boat, catch fish)*
4. How did the accident change the grandfather? *(injured him, made him sad)*
5. Why did Brian want to sit close to his grandfather? *(to get to know him better, to share stories, to share laughter)*
6. What do you think Brian will discover about his grandfather?

Story 5D

1. What animal has no heart? *(jellyfish)*
2. What are some features of a jellyfish? *(no heart, no brain, no skeleton, bell-shaped)*
3. What would happen if jellyfish has a skeleton? *(they would be rigid and/or sturdy)*
4. Why are jellyfish called "jellyfish?" *(no skeleton, 97% water)*
5. How does a jellyfish move? *(floats on ocean surface—blown by wind; floats under the ocean surface—pumps water in and out)*
6. Would you like to learn more about jellyfish?

Story 6A

1. Where do cowbirds live? (*North and South America*)
2. What are some of their characteristics? *(big eggs, push other babies out, don't build nests)*

3. Why do cowbird babies push other babies out of the nest? (*to have more room, to get all the food from the parent birds*)
4. Why don't the parents notice the baby cowbirds? (*too busy getting food, assumption that any baby must be their baby*)
5. Why don't adult cowbirds build their own nests? (*easier to take advantage of other species of birds*)
6. What do you think about cowbirds?

Story 6B
1. What animal has been around for millions of years? (*rhinoceros*)
2. What are some species of rhinos? (*Black, White, Javan, Sumatran, Indian*)
3. Why do rhinos have horns? (*protection, fighting*)
4. Why are some species of rhinos endangered? (*killed solely for their horns*)
5. How could rhinos be protected? (*make killing illegal, stop trade, establish preserves*)
6. Why are rhinos so amazing?

Story 6C
1. What is a city? (*a large group of people living in a specific area*)
2. What are some other places in which people live? (*hamlets, towns, borough, village*)
3. Where else can people live besides cities? (*rural area, country*)
4. What is a job that requires lots of land? (*farming*)
5. What are some reasons why people live in cities? (*economic, family, services, security, attractions*)
6. Would you rather live in a city or rural area?

Story 6D
1. What type of legend was described in this story? (*Mayan*)
2. What types of animals came to the hummingbird wedding? (*spiders, butterflies*)

3. How was this wedding similar to human weddings? (*elaborate, beautiful, colorful*)

4. From where did the colors of the wedding come? (*feathers, webs, butterflies, sunlight*)

5. Why did the Mayans create this story? (*to explain the creation of a very beautiful creature*)

6. Why do people enjoy hummingbirds so much?

Reference

Bloom, B. J. et al. (1956). *Taxonomy of educational objectives handbook I: Cognitive domain.* New York: David McKay.

Matching Books and Readers: Leveled Titles

THIS RESOURCE IS DESIGNED TO PROVIDE you with the specific tools you need to successfully implement and promote guided reading throughout your reading curriculum. One element that will have a significant impact on the success of your program is the match between books and students. By matching the reading ability of students with the reading level of books, you can help ensure that students (individually and collectively) are working with materials that are appropriate for their instructional needs. By the same token, as students' reading abilities increase, you can match them to increasingly more challenging books.

On the next several pages you will find various lists of children's literature. These books have been carefully categorized into the following 16 different levels:

3A = low third-grade level (3.0–3.2)	**5A** = low fifth-grade level (5.0–5.2)
3B = low third-grade level (3.3–3.4)	**5B** = low fifth-grade level (5.3–5.4)
3C = high third-grade level (3.5–3.7)	**5C** = high fifth-grade level (5.5–5.7)
3D = high third-grade level (3.8–3.9)	**5D** = high fifth-grade level (5.8–5.9)
4A = low fourth-grade level (4.0–4.2)	**6A** = low sixth-grade level (6.0–6.2)
4B = low fourth-grade level (4.3–4.4)	**6B** = low sixth-grade level (6.3–6.4)
4C = high fourth-grade level (4.5–4.7)	**6C** = high sixth-grade level (6.5–6.7)
4D = high fourth-grade level (4.8–4.9)	**6D** = high sixth-grade level (6.8–6.9)

The titles included in these lists are those most often used and/or recommended by intermediate grade teachers. They have been selected from a variety of sources, including recommendations from classroom teachers, reading supervisors, administrators, librarians (school and public), professional journals and periodicals (*Book Links, Horn Book, The Advocate*), children's literature textbooks, and major children's literature awards lists (Newbery, Caldecott, Horn Book, Coretta Scott King). They represent all eight genres of children's literature, a diversity of authors and illustrators, a range of interests, narrative and expository selections, and a variety of old "classics" and new favorites.

The titles were arranged in these categories simply because most intermediate teachers are quite comfortable with grade level designations and can easily adapt these levels to the reading materials already in their classrooms. However, this leveling process is influenced by factors other than simple grade level designations. In determining the appropriate and proper placement of a book within a specific category (such as 3B, 4D, 5A, and so on) other significant factors were also considered, including the following:

- the vocabulary difficulty of a specific book
- the length of the book (number of words and number of pages)
- the number of illustrations in relation to the amount of text
- the difficulty of the concepts
- the format of a book (such as typography and text layout)

Although the assignment of a book to a specific list has been done carefully and judiciously, it is important that you consider students' personal factors when selecting the reading material for one or more individuals. These include, but are not limited to:

- interest level(s) of individual students
- background knowledge of individual readers
- motivation to learn from text
- a diversity of literary genres
- opportunities for multicultural exploration
- favorite authors
- favorite book characters
- length of books
- balance between illustrations and text
- balance between narrative and expository writing

The consideration of these factors personalizes the matching of reader to material. This is done, not just in terms of grade level designations, but also in terms of the needs, interests, and attitudes of individual readers in your classroom.

Consider these lists as evolving lists. That is, feel free to add your own favorite titles to these lists on an ongoing basis. As new titles are published or reviewed in the various teacher magazines to which you subscribe, you can add them to this listing of books. Work with other colleagues at your grade level to add books to these lists throughout the school year. Stay in touch with the school librarian as well as the children's department at your local public library for suggestions on additions to these lists. Visit your local bookstore to stay up to date on the latest publications and most current literature. Attend seminars, workshops, and conferences on reading or children's literature to obtain "up-to-the-minute" ideas and suggestions on the availability and use of new titles.

The grade-level lists here include titles that are appropriate for students at specific ability levels to read in a guided reading program. That certainly does not mean that they cannot be used in other arenas of the overall reading program. For example, you will certainly discover titles appropriate for reading aloud as well as other titles that students can self-select for sustained silent reading times. Keep in mind that it is important to expose students to a wide range of books across the entire reading curriculum. These lists are appropriate starting points for the various dimensions of your reading program and individual students in your classroom.

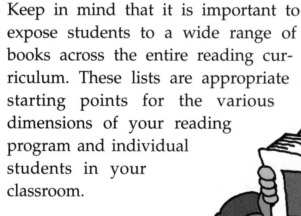

Third Grade

Low Third (3A)

The Amazing Bone. Steig, William. New York: Farrar, Straus and Giroux, LLC, 1983.

Amber Brown (series). Danziger, Paula. Old Greenwich: Listening Library.

Animal Dads. Collard, Sneed. Boston: Houghton Mifflin, 1997.

Antarctica. Cowcher, Helen. London: Milet Limited, 1997.

Big Al. Clements, Andrew. New York: Aladdin Paperbacks, 1997.

The Biggest Bear. Ward, Lynd. New York: Houghton Mifflin, 1988.

Busybody Nora. Hurwitz, Johanna. New York: HarperCollins, 2001.

Cam Jansen (series). Adler, David. New York: Penguin Putnam.

The Cat in the Hat. Seuss, Dr. New York: Random House, 1999.

The Cats' Burglar. Parish, Peggy. Madison: Turtleback Books, 1998.

A Chair for My Mother. Williams, Vera B. Madison: Turtleback Books, 1998.

Commander Toad (series). Yolen, Jane. New York: The Putnam Publishing Group.

Corduroy. Freeman, Don. New York: Viking Penguin, 1997.

Dandelion. Freeman, Don. New York: Puffin Books, 1977.

The Enormous Crocodile. Dahl, Roald. New York: Alfred A. Knopf, 2000.

Flat Stanley. Brown, Jeff. Madison: Turtleback Books, 1996.

Francis (series). Hoban, Russell. New York: HarperCollins.

Freckle Juice. Blume, Judy. New York: Houghton Mifflin, 1995.

Frogs. Gibbons, Gail. New York: Holiday House, 1993.

Germs Make Me Sick. Berger, Melvin. Madison: Turtleback Books, 1995.

The Giving Tree. Silverstein, Shel. New York: HarperCollins, 1994.

Grandfather's Journey. Say, Allen. New York: Houghton Mifflin, 1993.

Henry and Ribsy. Cleary, Beverly. New York: Morrow/Avon, 1990.

Horrible Harry (series). Kline, Suzy. New York: Penguin Putnam.

I'm in Charge of Celebrations. Baylor, Byrd. Madison: Turtleback Books, 1995.

Is This a House for Hermit Crab? McDonald, Megan. Madison: Turtleback Books, 1993.

Jimmy's Boa and the Big Splash Birthday Bash. Noble, Trinka Hakes. New York: Penguin Putnam, 1993.

The Jolly Postman. Ahlberg, Janet. Boston: Little, Brown, 1986.

Kitty in the Middle. Delton, Judy. New York: Houghton Mifflin, 1979.

Little House in the Big Woods. Wilder, Laura Ingalls. New York: HarperCollins, 1990.

The Magic Finger. Dahl, Roald. New York: Penguin Putnam, 1998.

Make Way for Ducklings. McClosky, Robert. New York: Penguin Putnam, 1999.

A Medieval Feast. Aliki. New York: HarperCollins, 1986.

Millions of Cats. Ga'g, Wanda. New York: Penguin Putnam, 1996.

The Mitten: A Ukrainian Folktale. Brett, Jan. New York: Putnam, 1998.

The Most Wonderful Doll in the World. McGinley, Phyllis. New York: Scholastic, 1992.

The Napping House. Wood, Audrey. San Diego: Harcourt, 2000.

Nate the Great (series). Sharmot, Marjorie. New York: Bantam Doubleday Dell.

Nettie's Trip South. Turner, Ann. Paramus, NJ: The Center for Applied Research in Education, 1998.

The One in the Middle Is the Green Kangaroo. Blume, Judy. New York: Bantam Doubleday Dell, 1988.

A Pocket for Corduroy. Freeman, Don. New York: Viking Penguin, 1997.

The Polar Express. Van Allsburg, Chris. New York: Houghton Mifflin, 1985.

Ramona the Brave. Cleary, Beverly. Madison: Turtleback Books , 1995.

Shooting Stars. Branley, Franklin M. New York: HarperCollins, 1991.

Slugs. Fredericks, Anthony D. Minneapolis: Learner Publishing, 2000.

Sun up, Sun Down. Gibbons, Gail. San Diego: Harcourt, 1987.

Tales of a Fourth Grade Nothing. Blume, Judy. Old Greenwich: Listening Library, 1996.

A Taste of Blackberries. Smith, Doris B. New York: HarperCollins, 1988.

The Teacher from the Black Lagoon. Thaler, Mike. New York: Scholastic, 1989.

Why Mosquitoes Buzz in People's Ears. Aardema, Verna. San Antonio, TX: Novel Units, Inc., 1999.

Whingdingdilly. Peet, Bill. New York: Houghton Mifflin, 1982.

Zebras. Fredericks, Anthony D. Minneapolis: Learner Publishing, 2000.

Low Third (3B)

Ant Cities. Dorros, Arthur. Madison: Turtleback Books, 1987.

The Chocolate Touch. Catling, Patrick S. New York: Bantam Doubleday Dell, 1998.

The Egyptian Cinderella. Climo, Shirley. Madison: Turtleback Books, 1992.

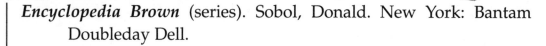

Encyclopedia Brown (series). Sobol, Donald. New York: Bantam Doubleday Dell.

Gregory, the Terrible Eater. Sharmot, Mitchell. Yardley: Checkerboard Press, 1987.

Imogene's Antlers. Small, David. New York: Alfred A. Knopf, 2000.

Ira Sleeps Over. Waber, Bernard. New York: Houghton Mifflin, 1987.

Jenius the Amazing Guinea Pig. King-Smith, Dick. New York: Hyperion, 1996.

John Henry: An American Legend. Keats, Ezra Jack. New York: Alfred A. Knopf, 1987.

Johnny Appleseed. Kellogg, Steven. New York: Morrow/Avon, 1988.

Mike Fink. Kellogg, Steven. Madison: Turtleback Books, 1998.

Miss Rumphius. Cooney, Barbara. New York: Viking/Penguin, 1982.

Pee Wee Scouts (series). Delton, Judy. New York: Bantam Doubleday Dell.

Plants That Never Ever Bloom. Heller, Ruth. New York: Penguin Putnam, 1999.

A Pocket for Corduroy. Freeman, Don. New York: Viking Penguin, 1997.

The Post Office Book. Gibbons, Gail. New York: HarperCollins, 1982.

The Reason for a Flower. Heller, Ruth. New York: Penguin Putnam, 1999.

Sam, Bangs, and Moonshine. Ness, Evaline. New York: Henry Holt & Co., 1995.

Sarah, Plain and Tall. MacLachlan, Patricia. New York: HarperCollins, 1996.

Sleeping Ugly. Yolen, Jane. New York: Penguin Putnam, 1997.

Tikki Tikki Tembo. Mosel, Arlene. New York: Henry Holt and Co., 1995.

The True Story of the Three Little Pigs. Scieszka, Jon. New York: Penguin, 1989.

Umbrella. Yashima, Taro. Madison: Turtleback Books, 1985.

Watch Out, Ronald Morgan! Giff, Patricia Reilly. New York: Penguin Putnam, 1986.

When Clay Sings. Baylor, Byrd. New York: Aladdin Paperbacks, 1987.

Wild Wild Sunflower Child Anna. Carlstrom, Nancy White. Madison: Turtleback Books, 1991.

The Winged Colt of Casa Mia. Byars, Betsy C. New York: Morrow/Avon, 1981.

The following titles from Rigby's *Literacy 2000 Guided Reading* series of books are also at this level:

Alfie's Gift	*In the Clouds*
All About Donkeys	*King Beast's Birthday*
Another Day, Another Challenge	*The Lucky Feather*
The Boy Who Cried Wolf	*Marcella*
Can I Have a Dinosaur?	*Oh, What a Daughter!*
Crocodilians	*Rabbit Stew*
Donkey	*Sam's Glasses*
The Dragon's Birthday	*The Spider and the King*
The Duck in the Gun	*Spider Man*
Four-legged Friends	*Trees Belong to Everyone*
Hello Creatures!	*The Very Thin Cat of Alloway Road*
Huberta the Hiking Hippo	*Who Pushed Humpty?*

High Third (3C)

Alexander and the Terrible, Horrible, No Good, Very Bad Day. Viorst, Judith. Woodstock: Dramatic Publishing, 2000.

Alexander, Who Used to Be Rich Last Sunday. Viorst, Judith. Topeka: Econo-Clad Books, 1999.

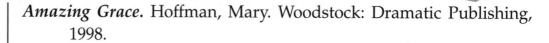

Amazing Grace. Hoffman, Mary. Woodstock: Dramatic Publishing, 1998.

And to Think That I Saw It on Mulberry Street. Seuss, Dr. New York: Random House, 1997.

Aunt Flossie's Hats (and Crab Cakes Later). Howard, Elizabeth F. New York: Houghton Mifflin, 1998.

The Beast in Ms. Rooney's Room. Giff, Patricia Reilly. New York: Bantam Doubleday Dell, 1996.

Best Friends. Kellogg, Steven. New York: Penguin Putnam, 1990.

The BFG. Dahl, Roald. Hampton: Chivers North America, 1999.

Black Beauty. Sewell, Anna. New York: Dorling Kindersley, 2000.

The Black Snowman. Mendez, Phil. New York: Scholastic, 1991.

Boxcar Children (series). Warner, Gertrude. Morton Grove: Albert Whitman and Co.

Bunnicula: A Rabbit Tale of Mystery. Howe, James. New York: Atheneum, 1999.

Class Clown. Hurwitz, Johanna. New York: Scholastic, 1988.

Cloudy with a Chance of Meatballs. Barrett, Judi. New York: Macmillan, 1978.

Crow Boy. Yashima, Taro. Madison: Turtleback Books, 1983.

The Five Chinese Brothers. Bishop, Claire H. New York: Penguin Putnam, 1996.

Fly Away Home. Bunting, Eve. New York: Clarion, 1991.

Frederick. Lionni, Leo. New York: Lectorum Publications, 1998.

The Frog Prince, Continued. Scieszka, Jon. New York: Penguin Putnam, 1994.

Henry and Beezus. Cleary, Beverly. New York: Morrow/Avon, 1990.

Henry and the Clubhouse. Cleary, Beverly. New York: Morrow/Avon, 1990.

Henry Higgins. Cleary, Beverly. Madison: Turtleback Books, 1996.

How the Grinch Stole Christmas. Seuss, Dr. New York: Random House, 1999.

It Could Always Be Worse. Zemach, Margot. New York: Farrar, Straus and Giroux, 1990.

Jack and the Beanstalk. Kellogg, Steven. New York: Morrow/Avon, 1997.

Jenny Archer (series). Conford, Ellen. New York: Little, Brown.

Jumanji. Van Allsburg, Chris. New York: Scholastic, 1996.

Junie B. Jones (series). Park, Barbara. New York: Random House.

Key to the Treasure. Parish, Peggy. New York: Bantam Doubleday Dell, 1980.

The Lorax. Seuss, Dr. New York: Random House, 1992

Madeline (series). Bemelmans, Ludwig. New York: Penguin Putnam.

Magic School Bus (series). Cole, Joanna. New York: Scholastic.

Matilda. Dahl, Ronald. Hampton: Chivers North America, 1999.

Matthew's Dream. Lionni, Leo. Madison: Turtleback Books, 1995.

Mike Mulligan and His Steam Shovel. Burton, Virginia L. New York: Houghton Mifflin, 1987.

More Stories Julian Tells. Cameron, Ann. Madison: Turtleback Books, 1986.

Much Ado About Aldo. Hurwitz, Johanna. Madison: Turtleback Books, 1989.

Nana Upstairs and Nana Downstairs. De Paola, Tomie. New York: Penguin Putnam, 2000.

Nettie Jo's Friends. McKissack, Patricia C. New York: Alfred A. Knopf, 1989.

No One Is Going to Nashville. Jukes, Mavis. New York: Alfred A. Knopf, 1987.

Only One Woof. Herriot, James. Madison: Turtleback Books, 1993.

Otherwise Known as Sheila the Great. Blume, Judy. New York: Dell, 1983.

The Popcorn Book. De Paola, Tomie. New York: Holiday House, 1978.

Ramona Forever. Cleary, Beverly. New York: Lectorum Publications, 1996.

Ramona the Pest. Cleary, Beverly. New York: Morrow/Avon, 1992.

Red Leaf, Yellow Leaf. Ehlert, Lois. San Diego: Harcourt, 1991.

The Relatives Came. Rylant, Cynthia. Madison: Turtleback Books, 1993.

Ribsy. Cleary, Beverly. Madison: Turtleback Books, 1996.

Runaway Ralph. Cleary, Beverly. New York: Morrow/Avon, 1991.

The Salamander Room. Mazer, Anne. New York: Knopf, 1991.

Stone Fox. Gardiner, John R. New York: HarperCollins, 1996.

The Story About Ping. Flack, Marjorie. New York: Penguin Putnam, 2000.

Strawberry Girl. Lenski, Lois. Madison: Turtleback Books, 1995.

A Turkey for Thanksgiving. Bunting, Eve. New York: Houghton Mifflin, 1995.

Tyler Toad and the Thunder. Crowe, Robert. New York: Penguin Putnam, 1992.

The Velveteen Rabbit. Williams, Margery. New York: Simon and Schuster, 1994.

High Third (3D)

Amos and Boris. Steig, William. New York: Penguin Putnam, 1977.

Berlioz the Bear. Brett, Jan. Madison: Turtleback Books, 1996.

Black and White. Macaulay, David. New York: Houghton Mifflin, 1990.

Chicken Sunday. Polacco, Patricia. New York: Penguin Putnam, 1992.

Chrysanthemum. Henkes, Kevin. New York: Morrow/Avon, 1996.

Doctor De Soto. Steig, William. Madison: Turtleback Books, 1997.

Ellen Tebbits. Cleary, Beverly. Madison: Turtleback Books, 1990.

Batman: Exploring the World of Bats. Pringle, Laurence. New York: Scholastic, 1993.

Five Brave Explorers. Hudson, Wade. Madison: Turtleback Books, 1995.

Fossils Tell of Long Ago. Aliki. Madison: Turtleback Books, 1990.

The Four Gallant Sisters. Kimmel, Eric A. New York: Henry Holt and Co., 1995.

Galimoto. Williams, Karen L. Columbus: Varsity Reading Services, 1993.

The Girl Who Loved Wild Horses. Goble, Paul. New York: Aladdin, 1993.

The Great Kapok Tree. Cherry, Lynne. San Diego: Gulliver Books, 1990.

Hank the Cowdog (series). Erickson, John. New York: Puffin Books.

Hawk, I'm Your Brother. Baylor, Byrd. Madison: Turtleback Books, 1986.

Hide and Seek Fog. Tresselt, Alvin R. New York: Morrow/Avon, 1998.

Horton Hears a Who. Seuss, Dr. New York: Random House, 1996.

If I Ran the Zoo. Seuss, Dr. New York: Random House, 1980.

The Island-Below-the-Star. Rumford, James. Boston: Houghton Mifflin, 1998.

Just a Dream. Van Allsburg, Chris. New York: Houghton Mifflin, 1990.

The Legend of the Bluebonnet. De Paola, Tomie. New York: Penguin Putnam, 1996.

The Legend of the Indian Paintbrush. De Paola, Tomie. New York: Penguin Putnam, 1996.

Lon Po Po: A Red-Riding Hood Story from China. Young, Ed. New York: Philomel, 1989.

Marvin Redpost (series). Sachar, Louis. New York: Random House.

Matilda. Dahl, Roald. Hampton: Chivers North America, 1999.

Moses the Kitten. Herriot, James. Topeka: Econo-Clad Books, 1999.

My Great-Aunt Arizona. Houston, Gloria M. New York: HarperCollins, 1997.

One Day in the Tropical Rain Forest. George, Jean Craighead. New York: HarperCollins, 1995.

One Day in the Woods. George, Jean Craighead. New York: HarperCollins, 1995.

One Morning in Maine. McCloskey, Robert. Madison: Turtleback Books, 1976.

Our Teacher's Having a Baby. Bunting, Eve. New York: Houghton Mifflin, 1992.

Ox-Cart Man. Hall, Donald. Madison: Turtleback Books, 1983.

Patrick's Dinosaurs. Carrick, Carol. New York: Houghton Mifflin, 1993.

Perfect the Pig. Jeschke, Susan. Madison: Turtleback Books, 1996.

Prairie School. Lenski, Lois. New York: HarperCollins, 1951.

Ramona Quimby, Age 8. Cleary, Beverly. New York: Lectorum Publications, 1996.

Song and Dance Man. Ackerman, Karen. Madison: Turtleback Books, 1992.

Strega Nona. De Paola, Tomie. New York: Little Simon, 1997.

Through Grandpa's Eyes. MacLachan, Patricia. Madison: Turtleback Books, 1983.

Time Warp Trio (series). Scieszka, Jon. Old Greenwich: Listening Library.

The Trouble with Trolls. Brett, Jan. New York: Penguin Putnam, 1999.

The Twits. Dahl, Roald. New York: Penguin Putnam, 1998.

Two Bad Ants. Van Allsburg, Chris. New York: Houghton Mifflin, 1988.

What's the Big Idea, Ben Franklin? Fritz, Jean. New York: Putnam, 1999.

The following titles from Rigby's *Literacy 2000* *Guided Reading* series of books are also at this level:

Animals of the Ice and Snow	*Nature's Celebration*
The Ballad of Robin Hood	*Once When I Was Shipwrecked*
Bats	*Paul Revere's Ride*
Brith the Terrible	*The Present from Aunt Skidoo*
Claudine's Concert	*Shorty*
Double Trouble	*The Story of Amy Johnson*
The Drought Maker	*The Tale of Veruschka Babuschka*
The Fiddle and the Gun	*That's a Laugh!*
Gail and Me	*Trains*
The Golden Goose	*Treasure Hunting*
Hunting With My Camera	*What a Day!*
Making Friends on Beacon Street	*Whirlybirds*

Fourth Grade

Low Fourth (4A)

Arthur, For the Very First Time. MacLachlan, Patricia. New York: HarperCollins, 1989.

The Best Christmas Pageant Ever. Robinson, Barbara. New York: HarperCollins, 1997.

Fisherman and His Wife. Zemach, Margot. New York: Norton, 1966.

The Gold Cadillac. Taylor, Mildred D. New York: Viking Penguin, 1998.

The Iron Giant. Hughes, Ted. New York: Alfred A. Knopf, 1999.

Julian, Secret Agent. Cameron, Ann. Madison: Turtleback Books, 1988.

One Small Blue Bead. Baylor, Byrd. New York: Scribner, 1992.

The Reluctant Dragon. Grahame, Kenneth. Mahwah, NJ: Troll, 1997.

Sylvester and the Magic Pebble. Steig, William. Parsippany, NJ: Silver Burdett Press, 1992.

Teacher's Pet. Hurwitz, Johanna. New York: Scholastic, 1989.

The Trumpet of the Swans. White, E. B. New York: HarperCollins, 2000.

The War with Grandpa. Smith, Robert Kimmel. New York: Dell, 1995.

The Whipping Boy. Fleischman, Sid. San Diego: Harcourt, 1993.

Low Fourth (4B)

All About Sam. Lowry, Lois. New York: Bantam Doubleday Dell, 1989.

The Egyptian News: Boy King Murdered? Steele, Philip. Cambridge: Candlewick Press, 2000.

Fantastic Mr. Fox. Dahl, Roald. New York: Penguin Putnam,1998.

Henry and the Paper Route. Cleary, Beverly. Madison: Turtleback Books, 1990.

Koko's Kitten. Patterson, Francine. New York: Scholastic, 1987.

Misty of Chincoteague. Henry, Marguerite. New York: Simon and Schuster, 1997.

Oceans. Simon, Seymour. New York: Morrow, 1999.

The Remembering Box. Clifford, Eth. New York: Morrow/Avon, 1992.

School's Out. Hurwitz, Johanna. New York: Scholastic, 1992.

Shiloh. Naylor, Phyllis Reynolds. New York: Bantam Doubleday Dell, 1998.

Skinnybones. Park, Barbara. New York: Knopf, 1982.

Smoky Night. Bunting, Eve. San Diego, CA: Harcourt Brace, 1994.

Tar Beach. Ringgold, Faith. Madison: Turtleback Books, 1996.

The Wretched Stone. Van Allsburg, Chris. New York: Houghton Mifflin, 1991.

The following titles from Rigby's *Literacy 2000* *Guided Reading* series of books are also at this level:

Barney	*Pandora's Box*
The Birthday Disaster	*Rupert and the Griffin*
Casey's Case	*Secrets of the Desert*
Cassidy's Magic	*The Shady Deal*
Dear Future	*Song of the Mantis*
Errol the Peril	*Strange Meetings*
Get a Grip, Pip!	*Television Drama*
Glumly	*Time for Sale*
Helping the Hoiho	*To JJ from CC*
The Loch Ness Monster Mystery	*The Tree, the Trunk, and the Tuba*

High Fourth (4C)

After the Goat Man. Byars, Betsy C. Magnolia: Peter Smith Publishers, 1995.

Amazing Animals: Nature's Most Incredible Creatures. Fredericks, Anthony D. and Sneed Collard. Minnetonka, MN: NorthWord Press, 2000.

Babe the Gallant Pig. King-Smith, Dick. New York: Random House, 2000.

Beezus and Ramona. Cleary, Beverly. New York: Morrow/Avon, 1990.

Blue Heron. Avi. New York: Morrow/Avon, 1993.

Dear Mr. Henshaw. Cleary, Beverly. New York: Lectorum Publications, 1996.

The Five Hundred Hats of Bartholomew Cubbins. Seuss, Dr. New York: Vanguard Press, 1989.

Fudge-a-Mania. Blume, Judy. New York: Dell, 1992.

The Giver. Lowry, Lois. New York: Bantam Doubleday, 1993.

Holes. Sachar, Louis. New York: Farrar, Straus and Giroux, 1998.

In the Year of the Boar and Jackie Robinson. Lord, Bette Bao. Madison: Turtleback Books, 1986.

On the Banks of Plum Creek. Wilder, Laura Ingalls. New York: HarperCollins, 1976.

Rain Forest Secrets. Dorros, Arthur. New York: Scholastic, 1999.

A River Ran Wild: An Environmental History. Cherry, Lynne. San Diego, CA: Harcourt Brace, 1992.

Surprising Swimmers. Fredericks, Anthony D. Minnetonka: Creative Publishing International, 2000.

There's a Boy in the Girls' Bathroom. Sachar, Louis. New York: Alfred A. Knopf, 1997.

These Happy Golden Years. Wilder, Laura Ingalls. Madison: Turtleback Books, 1971.

The Voyage of the Frog. Paulsen, Gary. New York: Dell, 1989.

Weird Walkers. Fredericks, Anthony D. Minnetonka: Creative Publishing International, 2000.

Yeh-Shen: A Cinderella Story from China. Louie, Ai-Ling. Madison: Turtleback Books, 1996.

High Fourth (4D)

Buffalo Hunt. Freedman, Russell. New York: Holiday House, 1988.

The Celery Stalks at Midnight. Howe, James. Madison: Turtleback Books, 1984.

Class President. Hurwitz, Johanna. Madison: Turtleback Books, 1991.

Cousins in the Castle. Wallace, Barbara Brooks. Madison: Turtleback Books, 1997.

Cybil War. Byars, Betsy C. New York: Penguin Putnam, 1990.

From the Mixed-Up Files of Mrs. Basil E. Frankweiler. Konigsburg, E. L. New York: Aladdin, 1999.

Hurricanes: Earth's Mightiest Storms. Lauber, Patricia. New York: Scholastic, 1996.

Little House on the Prairie. Wilder, Laura Ingalls. New York: HarperCollins, 1999.

Maniac Magee. Spinelli, Jerry. New York: Little, Brown, 1999.

Mufaro's Beautiful Daughters. Steptoe, John. New York: Lothrop, Lee and Shepard, 1987.

Owls in the Family. Mowat, Farley. Madison: Turtleback Books, 1996.

Pedro's Journal. Conrad, Pam. New York: Scholastic, 1992.

Perloo the Bold. Avi. New York: Scholastic, 1999.

Sideways Stories from Wayside School. Sachar, Louis. New York: Morrow/Avon, 1978.

Freedom Train: The Story of Harriet Tubman. Sterling, Dorothy. Madison: Turtleback Books, 1954.

Superfudge. Blume, Judy. Madison: Turtleback Books, 1996.

The True Confessions of Charlotte Doyle. Avi. Saint Paul: Paradigm Publishing, 1999.

Wayside School Is Falling Down. Sachar, Louis. New York: Morrow/Avon, 1998.

Zucchini. Dana, Barbara. Madison: Turtleback Books, 1998.

The following titles from Rigby's *Literacy 2000* *Guided Reading* series of books are also at this level:

A Battle of Words
Brian's Brilliant Career
The Cat Burglar of Pethaven Drive
Eureka!
Fernitickles
Fortune's Friend
Horrible Hank
In Search of the Great Bears
It's a Frog's Life
It's All in Your Mind, James Robert
Many Happy Returns

The Matchbox
The Rainbow Solution
Ryan's Dog Ringo
The Secret of Kiribu Tapu Lagoon
Spider Relatives
Timedetectors
Timothy Whuffenpuffen-Whippersnapper
The Week of the Jellyhoppers
Wing High, Gooftah

Fifth Grade

Low Fifth (5A)

Aliens Ate My Homework. Coville, Bruce. New York: Pocket Books, 1993.

Canyons. Paulsen, Gary. New York: Bantam Doubleday Dell, 1990.

Clever Camouflagers. Fredericks, Anthony D. Minnetonka, MN: NorthWord Press, 1999.

Elephants for Kids. Fredericks, Anthony D. Minnetonka, MN: NorthWord Press, 1999.

The Family Under the Bridge. Carlson, Natalie S. New York: HarperCollins, 1989.

Gathering of Days: A Novel. Blos, Joan W. Madison: Turtleback Books, 1990.

Gentle Ben. Morey, Walt. Madison: Turtleback Books, 1992.

James and the Giant Peach. Dahl, Roald. New York: Penguin, 1961.

Mississippi Bridge. Taylor, Mildred D. New York: Penguin Putnam, 2000.

Mr. Tucket. Paulsen, Gary. New York: Random House, 2000.

The Summer of the Swans. Byars, Betsy C. New York: Scholastic, 1997.

Low Fifth (5B)

Animal Sharpshooters. Fredericks, Anthony D. New York: Franklin Watts, 1999.

The Barn. Avi. New York: Morrow/Avon, 1996.

The Black Stallion. Farley, Walter. New York: Random House, 2000.

Bridge to Terabithia. Paterson, Katherine. New York: Harper & Row, 1989.

The Cay. Taylor, Theodore. New York: Doubleday, 1987.

Dear Mr. Henshaw. Cleary, Beverly. New York: Morrow, 1983.

Dogsong. Paulsen, Gary. New York: Aladdin, 2000.

Freaky Friday. Rodgers, Mary. New York: HarperCollins, 1977.

My Teacher Fried My Brains. Coville, Bruce. New York: Pocket Books, 1991.

My Teacher Is an Alien. Coville, Bruce. New York: Simon and Schuster, 1999.

Number the Stars. Lowry, Lois. Madison: Turtleback Books, 1998.

Ralph S. Mouse. Cleary, Beverly. New York: Morrow/Avon, 1993.

Skinnybones (series). Park, Barbara. Madison: Turtleback Books.

Two Under Par. Henkes, Kevin. New York: Viking Penguin, 1997.

High Fifth (5C)

A Blossom Promise. Byars, Betsy C. New York: Delacorte Press, 1987.

Cannibal Animals: Animals That Eat Their Own Kind. Fredericks, Anthony D. New York: Franklin Watts, 1999.

Farmer Boy. Wilder, Laura Ingalls. New York: HarperCollins, 1989.

The Fighting Ground. Avi. Madison: Turtleback Books, 1987.

From Miss Ida's Porch. Belton, Sandra. Madison: Turtleback Books, 1998.

Island of the Blue Dolphins. O'Dell, Scott. New York: Bantam Books, 1999.

Island. Paulsen, Gary. Madison: Turtleback Books, 1988.

Justin Morgan Had a Horse. Henry, Marguerite. New York: Simon and Schuster, 1995.

On the Far Side of the Mountain. George, Jean Craighead. Madison: Turtleback Books, 1991.

Romeo and Juliet—Together (And Alive!) at Last. Avi. New York: Morrow/Avon, 1988.

The Rough-Faced Girl. Martin, Rafe. New York: Putnam's, 1992.

The Sign of the Beaver. Speare, Elizabeth George. New York: Bantam Books, 1999.

The Skull of Truth. Coville, Bruce. New York: Simon and Schuster, 1999.

Song of the Trees. Taylor, Mildred D. Madison: Turtleback Books, 1996.

Stuart Little. White, E. B. Miami: Santillana USA Publishing Company, 1995.

The Summer My Father Was Ten. Brisson, Pat. Honesdale, PA: Boyds Mill Press, 1998.

High Fifth (5D)

A Different Kind of Courage. Howard, Ellen. New York: Simon and Schuster, 1996.

Hatchet. Paulsen, Gary. New York: Puffin, 1987.

Jeremy Thatcher, Dragon Hatcher. Coville, Bruce. New York: Simon and Schuster, 1991.

The Lion, the Witch and the Wardrobe. Lewis, C. S. New York: HarperCollins, 2000.

Missing May. Rylant, Cynthia. New York: Dell, 1993.

Mrs. Frisby and the Rats of NIMH. O'Brien, Robert C. New York: Aladdin, 1999.

My Side of the Mountain. George, Jean Craighead. New York: Penguin Putnam, 1997.

Old Yeller. Gipson, Fred. Princess Ann: Yestermorrow, 1999.

One-Eyed Cat. Fox, Paula. New York: Aladdin, 2000.

The River. Paulsen, Gary. New York: Dell, 1995.

The Slave Dancer. Fox, Paula. Hudson: Pathways Publishing, 1998.

The Witches. Dahl, Roald. New York: Penguin Putnam, 1999.

A Wrinkle in Time. L'Engle, Madeleine. New York: Bantam Books, 1999.

Sixth Grade

Low Sixth (6A)

The Cabin Faced West. Fritz, Jean. New York: Penguin Putnam, 1987.

Cannibal Animals: Animals That Eat Their Own Kind. Fredericks, Anthony D. New York: Watts, 1999.

Come Sing, Jimmy Jo. Paterson, Katherine. Madison: Turtleback Books, 1995.

The Flunking of Joshua T. Bates. Shreve, Susan R. Madison: Turtleback Books, 1993.

Harriet the Spy. Fitzhugh, Louise. New York: Bantam Doubleday Dell, 2000.

Harry Potter (series). Rowling, J. K. New York: Scholastic.

The Indian in the Cupboard. Banks, Lynne Reid. New York: Morrow/Avon, 1999.

My Teacher Glows in the Dark. Coville, Bruce. New York: Pocket Books, 1991.

Pigs Might Fly. King-Smith, Dick. Magnolia: Peter Smith Publishers, 2000.

Switching Well. Griffin, Peni R. Madison: Turtleback Books, 1994.

The Witch of Blackbird Pond. Speare, Elizabeth George. New York: Dell, 1997.

Low Sixth (6B)

Anastasia Krupnik. Lowry, Lois. New York: Bantam Doubleday Dell, 1998.

Cat Running. Snyder, Zilpha Keatley. New York: Dell, 1996.

The Cricket in Times Square. Seldon, George. New York: Bantam Books, 1999.

The Midnight Fox. Byars, Betsy C. New York: Penguin Putnam, 1981.

The Phantom Tollbooth. Juster, Norton. New York: Random House, 2000.

The Pigman. Zindel, Paul. New York: Bantam Doubleday Dell, 1983.

Sadako and the Thousand Paper Cranes. Coerr, Eleanor. New York: Putnam's, 1977.

Sing Down the Moon. O'Dell, Scott. New York: Dell, 1997.

Summer of the Monkeys. Rawls, Wilson. New York: Bantam Doubleday Dell 1998.

A Swiftly Tilting Planet. L'Engle, Madeleine. New York: Dell, 1986.

The Tower Trick. Stine, Megan. Littleton: Sundance Publishing, 1993.

Tuck Everlasting. Babbitt, Natalie. New York: Houghton Mifflin, 1995.

High Sixth (6C)

The Egypt Game. Snyder, Zilpha Keatley. New York: Dell, 1997.

The Hobbit. Tolkien, J. R. R. New York: Houghton Mifflin, 1999.

Mr. Popper's Penguins. Atwater, Richard. New York: Dell, 1992.

The Rescuers. Sharp, Margery. New York: Little, Brown, 1994.

Where the Red Fern Grows. Rawls, Wilson. New York: Random House, 2000.

High Sixth (6D)

Child of the Owl. Yep, Laurence. New York: HarperCollins, 1990.

Sounder. Armstrong, William H. New York: HarperCollins, 1996.

Tornadoes. Simon, Seymour. New York: Avon/Morrow, 1999.

We Are Witnesses: Five Diaries of Teenagers Who Died in the Holocaust. Boas, Jacob. New York: Scholastic, 1996.

The Wolves of Willoughby Chase. Aiken, Joan. Magnolia: Peter Smith Publishers, 1989.

Guided Reading Strategies

GUIDED READING RESTS on the notion that children's literature can and should be woven throughout the elementary curriculum. It seems likely, then, that you will want to use that literature in ways that stimulate reading development and conceptual understandings in a host of contexts. The following techniques and strategies are both exciting and dynamic, not only in terms of specific books and reading selections, but also in terms of the overall impact of your guided reading program. Periodically, you will be able to see how selected strategies have been used effectively by various classroom teachers from around the country. Please use their experiences as models for the implementation of specific strategies into your guided reading program.

Understandably, these ideas should not be used with a single book or group of books. Instead, the intent is to offer you a selection from which you can choose and begin to build meaningful and lasting experiences with all sorts of literature—with single guided reading groups or multiple groups. This is not a finite list but, rather, a collection of successful strategies used by teachers just like you. Here you can begin to create dynamic lesson plans that assist your students in becoming competent and energetic readers.

Before Reading Strategies

The strategies that follow are appropriate to use in guided reading sessions before reading a book. They are designed to help students activate their background knowledge and begin to draw connections between what they know and what they can know. You will also read about how selected strategies have been used effectively by various classroom teachers around the country, and you are invited to use their experiences as models for the implementation of one or more strategies in your lesson plans.

Here is a fascinating collection of classroom-tested and teacher-approved ideas for your classroom and your reading program. This text offers you a selection from which you can choose and begin to build meaningful and lasting experiences with all genres of literature. These suggestions are starting points from which you can create dynamic guided reading lessons that assist your students in becoming competent and energetic readers.

▶ Divergent Semantic Webbing

One method used as a framework for making linkages between prior knowledge and knowledge encountered in text is Semantic Webbing. Semantic Webbing is a graphic display of students' words, ideas, and images in concert with textual words, ideas, and images. A Semantic Web helps students comprehend text by activating their background knowledge, organizing new concepts, and discovering the relationships between the two. A Divergent Semantic Web includes the following steps:

1. Select a word or phrase central to the story and write it on the chalkboard.

2. Encourage students to think of as many words as they can that relate to the central word. These can be recorded on separate sheets or on the chalkboard.

3. Ask students to identify categories that encompass one or more of the recorded words.

4. Write category titles on the board. Students then share words from their individual lists or the master list appropriate for each category. Write words under each category title.

5. Students discuss and defend their word placements. Ask students to make predictions about story content.

6. After the story has been read, students can add new words or categories to the web. They can also modify other words or categories depending upon the information gleaned from the story.

See page 221 for a sample lesson plan using this strategy.

An Inside Look Harris Motha uses semantic webbing throughout his guided reading lessons for individual books he wishes to explore with his students. For the book *Hatchet* by Gary Paulsen (New York: Simon and Schuster, 2000), Harris writes the word *Survival* on the chalkboard and invites the students in a guided reading group of six individuals to brainstorm for all the words and concepts they know about survival. After the chalkboard is covered with words, Harris invites students to work in two small mini-groups to organize the words into several selected categories and to provide a title for each category. Afterward, Harris asks each mini-group to record their categories on the board and to explain their choice of words within groupings to the entire class. Discussion then centers on selecting the most representative categories. Students develop a "Master Web," which one student draws on the chalkboard. They write the identified category titles in white chalk and they write the items selected for each category on the radiating spokes in yellow chalk. During the course of the book, as students read about Brian's exploits, they add more words and ideas to the "Master Web" in pink chalk. Thus, students are able to see the relationships that can exist between their background knowledge (yellow chalk) and the knowledge they are learning within the book (pink chalk).

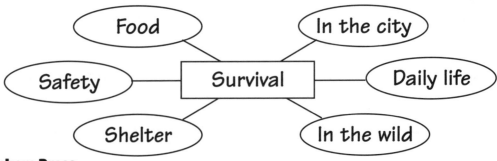

▶ Convergent Semantic Webbing

A Convergent Semantic Web differs from the divergent form in that several important concepts from a book are *pre-selected* by the teacher. The teacher writes each of these concepts into a structured web format and shares them with students before reading the book. Students tap into their background knowledge by adding words or phrases to the web in accordance with the pre-selected concepts. In most cases, Convergent Webbing is used with nonfiction materials.

Convergent Semantic Webbing is much more challenging for most students. This is because the categories or concepts have been pre-selected by the teacher. The selection process is based upon what the teacher considers to be the most important concepts within a book, concepts that may or may not have roots in the background knowledge of students. Thus, this strategy works when the teacher is assured that students within a guided reading group have the necessary background information to deal with a selected book. In cases where the teacher is unsure or when she or he knows students may have limited experiential backgrounds, Divergent Semantic Webbing is recommended.

Both Divergent and Convergent Webbing provide students with unique opportunities to consider what they know about a book before they read that book. Equally important is the fact that students are creating graphic representations of the information they bring to a text and the information they take away from a text. The connections between the two provide an effective "bridge" for comprehension and appreciation of all types of textual materials.

An Inside Look In preparation for reading the book *Cannibal Animals: Animals That Eat Their Own Kind* by Anthony D. Fredericks (New York: Watts, 1999), Mindy Rumsford tells a small group of her students that soon they are going to read a book about cannibalistic animals, survival, and obtaining food. She presents them with a diagram on the chalkboard of the convergent web on the following page.

Mindy then asks the students to tell what they know about "cannibalistic animals," "survival," and "obtaining food." She writes student responses around each of the appropriate categories on the group web.

Next, Mindy asks the students to make a prediction about what they think a book with the concepts "cannibalistic animals,"

```
         ┌─────────────────────────┐
         │   Cannibalistic animals │
     ┌───┤                         │
   ┌─┴─┐ └─────────────────────────┘       ┌──────────────────────┐
   │ ? ├─────────────────────────────────────┤      Survival       │
   └─┬─┘                                     └──────────────────────┘
     └───┐ ┌─────────────────────────┐
         │ │     Obtaining food      │
         └─┤                         │
           └─────────────────────────┘
```

"survival," and "obtaining food" might be about. Mindy records several predictions along one side of the chalkboard, and students select the one prediction they like the best. Mindy substitutes this prediction for the question mark on the web.

Mindy then encourages members of the group to read the book silently. When everyone is done, the group constructs a new web with the same three concepts. Students add ideas, facts, and information that they have learned while reading the book to the new web in the appropriate categories. Also, students talk about the main idea of the book and record that in the topmost circle. They compare the new web to the original web, and Mindy asks them to note any similarities and/or differences. 📖

▶ Student Motivated Active Reading Technique (S.M.A.R.T.)

S.M.A.R.T. is a comprehension strategy providing students opportunities to become personally involved in reading, both expository and narrative. Self-initiated questions and concept development underscore the utility of S.M.A.R.T. throughout a wide range of reading situations and abilities.

S.M.A.R.T., which is appropriate for individuals as well as small and large groups, can be organized as follows:

1. Choose a book, story, or reading selection for the group to discuss.

2. Record the title of the book on the chalkboard and encourage group members to ask questions about the title of the contents of the selection. Record all questions.

3. The group makes predictions about the content of the selection. Students decide on the questions they feel are most appropriate for exploration.

4. The group examines any illustrations found in the book or story and proposes additional questions. Students modify the initial prediction(s) according to information shared on the illustrations.

5. The group reads the selection (either orally or silently) and looks for answers to the recorded questions. Students may also generate new questions for discussion. As answers are found in the text, the individuals or group talk about them and attempt to arrive at agreeable responses.

6. Continue this procedure throughout the remainder of the selection: 1) seeking answers to previously generated questions and 2) continuing to ask additional questions. Upon completion of the book, the group discusses all recorded questions and answers provided in the selection and decides on all appropriate answers. The group also shares questions that were not answered from the text. Encourage students to refer back to the book to answer any lingering questions.

See page 215 for a sample lesson plan using this strategy.

▶ Quick Write

This strategy is particularly useful with expository or nonfiction materials. Not only does it allow students to tap into their background knowledge; it also provides them with active opportunities to generate their own self-initiated questions based on that knowledge. Here are the steps involved:

1. Prior to inviting students to read a nonfiction book, ask them to write (in paragraph form) everything they know about the topic of the book.

2. After a few minutes, ask students to revisit their respective paragraphs, inviting them to think of some questions about the topics generated by that paragraph. Invite them to record their questions on separate sheets of paper.

3. Provide group members with the titles of the chapters in the book, asking students to mark which questions on their respective lists they think will be answered in the book. Students may wish to assign a chapter number to a respective question on their sheet.

4. Give students an opportunity to share their questions and their predictions.

5. Invite students to read the book silently and to look for answers to their questions, if possible. After the reading, students may use any unanswered questions to stimulate group discussion or for independent research projects.

An Inside Look Maureen Thompson is ready to share the book *Animal Dads* by Sneed Collard with a small group of her third-grade students. She asks students to each write a short paragraph on everything they might know about fathers in the animal kingdom. After students have completed this initial activity, she invites them to create a series of questions related to their stories. They generate the following list:

I. How are animal dads like human dads?
2. What are some things animal dads do?
3. Are animal dads mean?
4. Do animal dads take care of their babies?
5. How do animal dads feed their babies?
6. What do animal dads teach their kids?

After some discussion, the group decides to focus on questions 1, 2, and 6. Maureen knows that that these questions will form what she calls a "predictive foundation" for their reading of the book. After the reading, discussion is centered on the answers students located as well as other questions that arose during the independent reading. As expected, the discussion is lively and animated as a result of the before-reading question-generating activity.

▶ Concept Cards

Concept cards allow students to tap their background knowledge about the topic of a book, share that information with classmates, and make predictions about the content of a piece of literature. At the same time, students can manipulate their vocabulary and share ideas related to word study and comprehension of text. Although this strategy works particularly well with nonfiction materials, it can also be used with narrative text.

1. Before students read a book, select 20 to 25 words from throughout the book. It is preferable to have words from the front, middle, and back of the book. Include words with which students are familiar, words essential to comprehension of text, and a few unknown words.

2. Print each set of words on index cards and distribute the set to a guided reading group.

3. Students assemble the cards into categories of their own choosing. (*Note:* Do not tell students a specific number of categories or the number of "word cards" that should be in each grouping.) Encourage students to place words in categories according to their own knowledge of those words or their predictions of how those words might be used in the forthcoming text.

4. Students share their various categories and grouping and provide a rationale for the placement of word cards within specific groups.

5. Students read the book, looking for the words on the index cards. After reading, encourage students to rearrange cards or manipulate words into new categories or groupings based on the information gleaned from the text. Afterward, invite students to discuss reasons for any rearrangements and compare placements with those they did in the pre-reading stage.

See page 274 for a sample lesson plan using this strategy.

An Inside Look As part of a science unit on African animals, Charlie Lessom, a fifth-grade teacher in Golden, Colorado, introduces his students to *Elephants for Kids* by Anthony D. Fredericks (Minnetonka, MN: NorthWord Press, 1999). (This book provides young readers with fascinating information about African and Asian elephants as narrated by a Kenyan boy.) In preparation for guided reading lessons with individual groups, Charlie prepares several sets of Concept Cards. He selects 25 words from the book and types each word on five separate index cards (thus creating five sets of 25 words each). Charlie selects words from throughout the book, including words known by his students as well as additional vocabulary important to their overall comprehension. The words in the following chart are those Charlie used with his students.

Kenya	bull	cow	species	India
savanna	gestation	forest	herd	calf
female	male	matriarch	leader	migration
memory	trunk	muscle	organ	pregnant
tusk	incisor	ivory	zoologist	herbivore

Charlie presents a group of four students (Barbara, Inez, Thomas, and Sam) with a set of Concept Cards and invites them to arrange their cards in categories of their own choosing. Afterward, he asks the group to discuss their categories and groupings with him. Discussion centered on some of the word groups students created and their rationale for assigning a word to a particular category.

Charlie then asks the group members to read the book silently, inviting them to watch for the words identified on the Concept Cards. Upon finishing the book, Charlie asks the students to rearrange and reassemble the cards according to the information they learned in the book. The students share and compare data and facts from the book. Charlie encourages students to discuss any differences between the arrangement of cards before the reading of the book and new arrangements made after they read the book. Students are amazed to discover the ways in which their background information could be combined with the book information to create a host of new categories and groupings. 📖

▶ Mental Imagery

Mental imagery is the creation of pictures in the reader's mind prior to, during, or after reading. (We will discuss this all-important strategy as a Before strategy.) However, with appropriate modifications and extension, you will be able to use this technique with all types of readers, all types of reading materials, and at all stages of the reading process.

A process of mental imagery helps readers construct "mind pictures" that serve as an aid in comprehension and as a way to tie together predictions, background knowledge, and textual knowledge in a satisfying experience. Once images are created (and colored by a reader's experiences) they become a permanent part of long-term memory. Just as important, they assist in the development of independent readers who are "connected" with the books they read.

It is important to note that mental imagery is more a developmental process than a single instructional strategy. In other words, students need to be exposed to four basic stages throughout the reading program (and throughout the school year) in order to effectively integrate mental imagery as a personal reading strategy. Following are the four basic stages of mental imagery along with some attendant activities:

1. Provide students with opportunities to create images of concrete and tangible objects.
- Visualize a three-dimensional object.
- Visualize a variety of objects.

2. Encourage students to visualize and recall familiar objects, scenes, or past experiences outside of the classroom.
- Visualize a familiar room (bedroom).
- Imagine playing with a favorite object.

3. Provide students with opportunities to listen to high-imagery stories that utilize common experiences or knowledge.
- Share an unfamiliar story with good description and action.
- Illustrate selected parts of a story.

4. At this stage students begin to create their own mental images as they read stories.

- Describe character emotions and feelings after guided reading.
- Explain potential scenery for a play.

Mental imagery works particularly well when the following guidelines are made part of the entire process:

1. Students need to understand that their images are personal and are affected by their own backgrounds and experiences.

2. There is no right or wrong image for any single student.

3. Students need sufficient opportunity to create their images prior to any discussion.

4. Students need adequate time to discuss the images they develop.

5. Assist students in image development using a series of open-ended questions (such as "Tell us more about your image" or "Can you add some additional details?")

See page 223 for a sample lesson plan using this strategy.

An Inside Look Imogene Rodriguez is a fourth-grade teacher in Modesto, California. She has been teaching for 11 years and has incorporated mental imagery in a variety of curricular activities. She has discovered that when students have sufficient opportunities to generate their own personal mental images prior to the reading of a book, their recall of significant events as well as their overall comprehension of the story increases significantly. "My mental imagery activities are fairly structured," Imogene states. "I don't use them for every book, but rather over the years I've been able to construct a variety of pre-reading imagery activities that help students 'get into' the theme or plot of a forthcoming book. Later, in our post-reading discussions, I find that students have a better grasp of the material and are more personally involved in it."

Following is a mental imagery activity Imogene uses just prior to having her students read the book *Holes* by Louis Sachar (New York: Farrar, Straus and Giroux, 1998):

Close your eyes. Create a picture in your mind of Texas. Imagine that you are standing in the middle of Texas. Imagine that you are standing in the middle of a very large and very dry lake bed. Imagine that you are standing in a wide open space. There are very few plants. There are no animals. The temperature is very hot. You are beginning to sweat. Everywhere you look, there is nothing but emptiness. There are no birds in the sky. There are no plants on the ground. Look carefully and you can see holes in this lake bed. Lots of holes. Everywhere you look there are holes. Each hole has been dug with a shovel. Beside each hole is a pile of dirt. Each hole is about four feet deep. It is hot. It is dry. You are thirsty. You have a shovel in your hand. You are digging a hole in the middle of a dry lake bed. Your hands hurt. Your shoulders hurt. You hurt all over. You want some water, but there is none. It is hot. It is very hot.

After reading this to students, Imogene invites them to open their eyes and describe the images each one created in her or his head. Imogene points out the similarities and differences in the images and notes how everyone's mental image was personal and colored by her or his own experiences. Then Imogene encourages students in a guided reading group to read the book *Holes*. When they are finished reading, Imogene provides opportunities for students to compare their pre-reading images with those depicted in the book. 📖

▶ K-W-L

K-W-L (Ogle, 1986) is a three-step framework that helps students access appropriate information in expository writing. It takes advantage of student's background knowledge and helps demonstrate relationships between that knowledge and the information in text.

K-W-L (What I Know, What I Want to Learn, What I Learned) involves students in three major cognitive steps: accessing their background knowledge about a topic, determining what students would like to learn about that subject, and evaluating what was learned about the topic. The following steps provide an outline through which teachers and students can begin to read expository text:

1. Invite students to talk about what they already know about the topic of the text. This information should be freely volunteered and written on the chalkboard (K, What We Know).

2. Encourage students to categorize the information they have volunteered. This can be done through various grouping strategies such as semantic webbing. These groupings can be recorded on the chalkboard.

3. Students make predictions about the types of information the text will contain. These predictions should be based on their background knowledge as well as the categories of information elicited in step 2.

4. Encourage students to generate their own questions about the text. These can be discussed and recorded in a section of the board entitled "W, What We Want to Find Out."

5. Students then read the text and record any answers to their questions. Students can do this individually or in pairs.

6. Upon completion of the text, provide students with an opportunity to discuss the information learned and how that data relates to their prior knowledge. The groups talks about questions for which no information was found in the text. Help students discover other sources for satisfying their inquiries.

See page 241 for a sample lesson plan using this strategy.

▶ Anticipation Guide

Anticipation Guides alert students to some of the major concepts in textual material before it is read. As such, students have an opportunity to share ideas and opinions as well as activate their prior knowledge about a topic before they read about that subject. It is also a helpful technique for eliciting students' misconceptions about a subject. Students become actively involved in the dynamics of reading a specified selection because they have an opportunity to talk about the topic before reading about it.

1. Read the story or selection and attempt to select the major concepts, ideas, or facts in the text. For example, in a selection on weather, you can identify the following concepts:

    a. There are many different types of clouds.

    b. Different examples of severe weather include tornadoes, hurricanes, and thunderstorms.

    c. Precipitation occurs in the form of rain, snow, sleet, and hailstones.

    d. Many types of weather occur along fronts.

2. Create five to ten statements (not questions) that reflect common misconceptions about the subject, are ambiguous, or are indicative of students' prior knowledge. Statements can be written on the chalkboard or photocopied and distributed.

3. Give students plenty of opportunities to agree or disagree with each statement. Whole-group or paired discussions would be appropriate. After discussions, let each individual student record a positive or negative response to each statement. Initiate discussions focusing on reasons for individual responses.

4. Invite students to read the text, keeping in mind the statements and their individual or group reactions to those statements.

5. After reading the selection, engage the group in a discussion on how the textual information may have changed their opinions. Provide students with an opportunity to record their reactions to each statement based upon what they read in the text. It is not important that they reach a consensus, nor that they agree with everything the author states. Rather, it is more important for students to engage in an active dialogue that allows them to react to the relationships between prior knowledge and current knowledge.

See page 255 for a sample lesson plan using this strategy.

An Inside Look It is late September, the height of the hurricane season in south Florida. Mary Anne Spangler's fifth graders are caught up in a whirlwind (pardon the pun) of weather-related activities as part of a combined science/language arts unit. A recent hurricane that had passed through the Caribbean had been front-page news in the *Miami Herald* for several days and had sparked students' curiosity about these natural disasters and how they form. Based on her students' interests, Mary Anne introduces one group of students to the book *Hurricanes: Earth's Mightiest Storms* by Patricia Lauber (New York: Scholastic, 1996). Before students read the book, Mary Anne prepares the following Anticipation Guide:

Name _____ Date _____

Directions: Look at the sentences on this page. The statements are numbered from 1 to 6. Read each sentence. If you think that what it says is correct, print *Yes* on the line under the word *Before*. If you think the sentence is wrong, print *No* on the line under the word *Before*. Do the same for each sentence. Remember how to do this, because you will do it again *after* you read the selection.

Before   After

_____   _____   **1.** Hurricanes happen throughout the world.

_____   _____   **2.** The greatest hurricane damage is done by a storm surge.

_____   _____   **3.** Hurricanes are named after women.

_____   _____   **4.** People fly airplanes into hurricanes.

_____   _____   **5.** Hurricane winds can be more than 200 m.p.h.

_____   _____   **6.** All hurricanes are dangerous.

Working as a group, five students (Clark, Andre, Jesus, Damian, and Caroline) respond to each of the statements on the Anticipation Guide. Group discussion centers on reasons for their choices and predictions about what they might discover in the book. Mary Anne then provides a copy of the book to each student and invites the group to read and locate confirming data related to each of the identified statements. Students then complete the *After* column of the guide and share their reasons for placing *Yes* or *No* on each line. Follow-up discussions reveal some differences of opinion, yet the conversation is lively as well as supportive. Students find that they each bring different perspectives to a book, yet they can all benefit from those differences in a mutually stimulating learning environment.

Anticipation Guides are also appropriate for use with fiction material. Note how the book *The Salamander Room* by Anne Mazer (New York: Knopf, 1991) could be developed into an anticipation guide. 📖

Name _____ Date _____

Directions: Look at the sentences on this page. The statements are numbered from 1 to 5. Read each sentence. If you think that what it says is correct, print *Yes* on the line under the word *Before*. If you think the sentence is wrong, print *No* on the line under the word *Before*. Do the same for each sentence. Remember how to do this because you will do it again *after* you read the book *The Salamander Room*.

Before   After

_____   _____   **1.** Salamanders live under dried leaves.

_____   _____   **2.** Most salamanders are orange in color.

_____   _____   **3.** Salamanders eat crickets and other insects for food.

_____   _____   **4.** The diet of salamanders is similar to the diet of frogs.

_____   _____   **5.** Salamanders are an important part of the ecology of the forest.

_____   _____   **6.** People should not remove animals from their natural habitat.

▶ Semantic Feature Analysis

This strategy provides opportunities for students to share ideas about word concepts and vocabulary words used in a piece of literature. It can assist students in making decisions about how words are related and it stimulates discussions about the features of both familiar and unfamiliar vocabulary. To implement this strategy:

1. Identify a major topic from a forthcoming book. Using the SFA Grid on page 112, select a category of words that can be described with multiple features (for example, the topic is Transportation; words could be *bus, motorcycle, airplane, barge, skateboard*, etc.;

features might be on land, on water, in the air, motorized, no wheels, four wheels, more than four wheels, etc.).

2. Invite students to brainstorm words that relate to the general category. These words should be listed down the left-hand side of the SFA Grid (for example, *bus, motorcycle*). Encourage students to brainstorm features of some of those words. These should be listed across the top of the Grid (for example, *on land, on water*).

3. Invite students to match a word with a feature by placing a + (match) or – (no match) in the place where a row and a column intersect.

4. Upon completion, invite students to discuss words with common features or features represented by more than one word. Encourage conversation about any agreements or disagreements.

Following is a filled-in example of an SFA Grid. A blank SFA Grid appears on page 112.

Sample SFA Grid

Topic: **Transportation**

Features

	On land	On water	In the air	On tracks	Motorized	Has wheels	
Motorcycle	+	–	–	–	+	+	
Airplane	–	–	+	–	+	+	
Barge	–	+	–	–	–	–	
Skateboard	+	–	–	–	–	+	
Bus	+	–	–	–	+	+	

An Inside Look Jon Lingenfelter has recently completed his first year of teaching third grade in Madison, Wisconsin. He knows the value of integrating vocabulary work throughout all dimensions of his reading program as well as his entire curriculum. He has discovered that the use of a Semantic Feature Analysis grid provides his students with opportunities to tap into their personal backgrounds of information and share their knowledge in a supportive format.

Just before initiating a new thematic unit on Transportation, in which Jon will share selected titles with students as part of a cross-curricular (reading and social studies) plan, he invites students in one of his guided reading groups to contribute several words about transportation. Jon writes each of these words down the left side of a master SFA grid. After recording several words, Jon asks the members of the group to discuss any similarities or differences among the words in terms of comparable concepts. He records pluses and minuses on the chart as students engage in an active "give and take" about the identified words. Jon takes a few minutes to illustrate some of the comparisons and invites students to watch for additional comparisons as they read the selected literature for the unit. In this case, Jon keeps the grid posted throughout the reading of several books. He encourages students to record, alter, modify, or change marks throughout each of the planned guided reading sessions with individual books. Near the conclusion of the unit, Jon plans time for the students to make any final modifications. He shows them how they have altered their initial concepts about Transportation throughout the reading of the designated books.

Name _____

Date _____

SFA Grid

Topic: _____

Features

▶ Reflective Sharing Technique

The Reflective Sharing Technique demonstrates the interrelationships that naturally exist between the language arts and specific curricular areas. This strategy stimulates children to use language as a basis for learning across the curriculum. The Reflective Sharing Technique encourages students to share and discuss ideas that are important to them while, at the same time, reacting in positive ways to each other. To use this technique, follow these steps:

1. Choose a book or story appropriate to the ability level of your students in a guided reading group of four individuals. Select the general subject area of the story and record it on the chalkboard.

2. For approximately three to five minutes, invite students to brainstorm for as many ideas concepts, or items that could be included in that subject area (see below). These items can be recorded on the chalkboard. Brainstorming should stimulate a free flow of ideas, without regard to quality. The emphasis should be on generating a quantity of ideas and a wide range of responses.

3. Ask each student to select one of the brainstormed ideas from the list on the board. Invite each student to write about his or her selected item for about five minutes (adjust this time limit according to the age or ability levels of students).

4. Sharing what each person has composed is the most important part of this activity.

   a. Assign students specific tasks (it is very important to have a group of four for the sharing process). In the group, members take specific roles:

   1) Person 1 reads what he or she wrote.

   2) Person 2 summarizes what Person 1 read.

   3) Person 3 tells what he or she liked about what Person 1 read.

   4) Person 4 tells something else he or she would like to know about the subject upon which Person 1 wrote.

Note: This completes Round 1.

b. After one round of sharing, the process is repeated until the group has completed four rounds and everyone has taken on all four roles (see the following chart).

Role	Round 1	Round 2	Round 3	Round 4
Reads what he or she wrote	Person 1	Person 2	Person 3	Person 4
Summarizes reader's story	Person 2	Person 3	Person 4	Person 1
Tells what he or she liked	Person 3	Person 4	Person 1	Person 2
Tells something else he or she wants to know	Person 4	Person 1	Person 2	Person 3

5. Point out to students the wealth of information they already have about the subject of the book or story even before they begin to read it. You may wish to invite students to discuss how their backgrounds of experience melded with ideas in the book.

6. At this point invite students to read the book independently.

Note: You may wish to conduct the Reflective Sharing Technique as an oral activity with some groups. Designate a student to talk about special interests. The rest of the group takes on the roles of summarizer, positive reactor, and those asking about other things they would like to know.

See page 246 for a sample lesson plan using this strategy.

▶ Picture Perfect

Picture Perfect is an exciting Before reading strategy that stimulates background experiences, ties them in with textual knowledge, and provides you with some relevant information upon which to design an effective reading lesson. Its other advantage is that it incorporates the writing process into the reading process and provides students a glimpse into the interrelationships that exist between the two. This strategy has been used effectively with all ability levels and all grade levels. Here's how it works:

1. Select an illustration, photograph, or picture from the cover or inside of a book. The illustration should provide sufficient clues or information about the book in terms of setting, characters, or significant events.

2. Make a transparency of the illustration and project it onto a screen.

3. Invite each group to look at the illustration and then generate three to five questions they have about the illustration. One person in the group records these questions for group members.

4. Invite each group to exchange their questions with another group.

5. Invite each group to now write a story that embeds answers to the other group's questions in that story. The story can be fiction or nonfiction, expository or narrative. All members of a group contribute elements of the story while one member records the story.

6. When the stories are completed, invite each group to return the story to the group that originated the questions.

7. Each group can now read the story that was written in response to members' questions.

8. Discuss the background knowledge that was tapped, as well as the information generated as a result of that background knowledge, in concert with the selected illustration.

9. Invite students (individually or collectively) to read the book.

10. After completing the book, students can compare the plot of the book with that of the stories.

11. Invite student groups to modify, alter, or adjust their Before Reading stories in light of the information in the book. What new information needs to be included in the second draft?

Picture Perfect has proven itself as an effective and lasting strategy that underscores students' active involvement and engagement in the guided reading process. There are no right or wrong ways to construct the initial stories, and those essays will be reflective of the prior experiences students bring to the reading of a book. That information will be helpful for you in directing and shaping the content of any follow-up lessons.

See page 219 for a sample lesson plan using this strategy.

▶ No Book DR-TA

The No Book DR-TA (Directed Reading-Thinking Activity; Gill & Bear, 1988) is an activity designed to elicit students' background knowledge. Based on an inquiry model of reading, No Book DR-TA offers you data on what students already know about a topic while helping students establish a purpose for exploring the body of knowledge to be presented. This strategy can be conducted with one or more guided reading groups. The following steps make up the No Book DR-TA:

1. Students in a guided reading group list everything they can think of that might pertain to a designated topic. Students may wish to generate ideas on their own or brainstorm as a group for all the background knowledge they have on a particular topic. A master list is maintained by the group.

2. Students group the items in their list into categories. (It may be necessary for you to model categorizing for students initially.)

3. Students assign a name to each group of items and arrange them as though they were a table of contents for a book. This should be done as a group activity until students have sufficient practice in assigning titles to their respective categories.

4. Invite each student to write a "book" about the upcoming topic using the categories as chapter titles. Encourage students to write as much about each topic as they can, summarizing what each section is about. If students get stuck, Allow them to make up what they don't know. Keep the "books" on file. Students can edit them as they read the actual piece of literature or rewrite them at the conclusion of the individual reading.

An Inside Look Chris Montgomery uses No Book DR-TA in her third-grade classroom. The literature selection is *Cloudy with a Chance of Meatballs* by Judy Barrett (New York: Macmillan, 1978). Chris wants to find out how much background knowledge students in the guided reading group have about the weather before asking them to read the book. The students in the group come up with the following list of data on "changes in the weather" during the first three steps of the No Book DR-TA:

Seasons	Hot Weather	Cold Weather	Temperature	In the Sky
Winter	sunny	snow	hot	clouds
Summer	warm	ice	warm	rain
Fall	sun		cool	lightning
Spring				cold

It is evident to Chris that the students in this group have some knowledge about the weather, although their backgrounds are not strong. After the students finish dictating a class book (which Chris records on chart paper), she invites all group members to read *Cloudy with a Chance of Meatballs*. At the conclusion of the reading, Chris invites students to write another "book" and compare it with the one generated using the No Book DR-TA. Students in the group are delighted to learn that some of their previous perceptions about the weather have changed. The discussions lead Chris to select a nonfiction weather book for the group to read on the following day, when students participate in the same steps and then compare their respective "books."

▶ Possible Sentences

Possible Sentences (Moore and Moore, 1986) is an exciting Before strategy that 1) assists students in learning new vocabulary, 2) generating appropriate story predictions, 3) developing individual (or group) purposes for reading, and 4) stimulating their intellectual curiosity about a book or story. It is a strategy appropriate for all types of expository material, this strategy revolves around a five-part lesson plan:

1. List essential vocabulary from the book. These words are pre-selected by you and may be presented to students on sheets of paper or on the chalkboard.

2. Students are invited to select at least two words from the list and construct a sentence—one they think might be in the book.

3. Ask each student to read the book in order to check the accuracy of the sentences generated.

4. Evaluate each of the sentences in terms of the information presented in the book. Sentences may be eliminated, revised, changed, altered, or modified in light of the information gleaned from the book. At times, students will need to reread portions of the book in order to confirm or alter their original predictions.

5. After the original sentences have been evaluated, students are encouraged to generate additional sentences using the selected vocabulary. As new sentences are generated, they are checked against the original story for accuracy.

Possible Sentences allows students to integrate important vocabulary and their predictive abilities in a worthwhile activity. This strategy assists students in developing connections between prior knowledge and textual knowledge while incorporating a variety of languaging skills. Although Possible Sentences was originally designed to help students focus on expository materials, it is equally successful with selected narrative books as well. In addition, it provides important pre-lesson assessment information that you can address later in the reading process.

See page 264 for a sample lesson plan using this strategy.

An Inside Look Sally Abrams is a third-grade teacher in Plattsburgh, New York. One day she assigns the book *Fly Away Home* by Eve Bunting to two separate guided reading groups. Before students read the book, she provides them with duplicated sheets on which she has typed the following terms:

airport	airlines
security	terminal
passengers	attendants
pilots	luggage
girder	sliding door
strangers	janitor
apartment	forever

Each student elects two words and constructs a sentence he or she thinks will be in the book. On the board Sally records each of the sentences volunteered by the students. Below are three sentences generated by students in one guided reading group:

There's lots of <u>passengers</u> and <u>luggage</u> at an <u>airport</u>.

<u>Pilots</u> fly <u>airlines</u> in and out of an <u>airport</u>.

<u>Strangers</u> walk through the <u>sliding door</u>.

Sally asks the students to each read the book in order to check the accuracy of the sentences generated. After the reading, the groups discuss the appropriateness of their sentences and Sally encourages them to generate additional sentences using the selected vocabulary. In this way, she helps her students understand the relationship of specific vocabulary words to the overall comprehension of a text.

▶ Story Impressions

One way you can assist your students in actively thinking about the materials they are to read is a reading strategy known as Story Impressions (McGinley and Denner, 1987). Story Impressions encourages students to engage in predictive activities utilizing key concepts pre-selected from a piece of literature. Its advantage lies in the fact that students have realistic opportunities to predict and confirm key elements from the plot of a story. Following are the steps involved in this strategy:

1. Select 10 to 15 key words, ideas, or phrases from a forthcoming book. These key concepts should represent the character, setting, and important points from the plot. These ideas should be printed in sequential order down the left-hand side of a sheet of paper. You may wish to draw an arrow between each listing.

2. Present the sheet to a guided reading group and tell students that the list represents important concepts from the book.

3. Invite students to read through the list (top to bottom) and encourage them to discuss how the ideas might be related or connect.

4. The group constructs a story with the brainstormed ideas. This can be recorded on chart-pack paper or on the chalkboard. As an individual activity, each student can be presented with a duplicated copy of the list of key concepts. Then each student records her or his original story on the right-hand side of the paper.

5. Students are encouraged to read the original book and then discuss how the stories compare. The object is *not* to have an exact match, but rather to see how a basic set of ideas can be interpreted differently by two separate "authors."

Below is a list of *Story Impression* key concepts that could be used for the book *The Great Kapok Tree* by Lynne Cherry.

Amazon rain forest
Kapok tree
Chopping tree
Man falls asleep
Animals whisper
Boa constrictor hissed
Troupe of monkeys
Jaguar growls in his ear
Unstriped anteater said
Child murmured
Man awoke
Walked out of rain forest

Student Story:

© 2001 Rigby

During Reading Strategies

In many cases, the During reading stage of guided reading will engage students in the silent reading of a book. This offers students opportunities to process information at their appropriate reading level. This is also a supportive time in which the teacher can assist or guide reading interpretations or comprehension.

Occasionally, you may wish to interject a reading strategy in order to help students experience success and make meaning from what they read. The following strategies can help make that a reality. As you read these listings, you will undoubtedly notice that several of these ideas would also be appropriate as Before and After strategies, too.

▶ Directed Reading-Thinking Activity (DRTA)

The DRTA (Stauffer, 1969) is a comprehension strategy that stimulates students' critical thinking of text. It is designed to allow students to make predictions, think about those predictions, verify or modify the predictions with text, and stimulate a personal involvement with many different kinds of reading material.

DRTAs are guided by three essential questions, which are inserted throughout the reading and discussion of a book. These include:

"What do you think will happen next?" (Using prior knowledge to form hypotheses)

"Why do you think so?" (Justifying predictions; explaining one's reasoning)

"How can you prove it?" (Evaluating predictions; gathering additional data)

Vacca and Vacca (1989) outline a series of general steps for the DRTA:

1. Begin with the title of the book or with a quick survey of the title, subheads, illustrations and so forth. Ask students, "What do you think this story (or book) will be about?" Encourage students to make predictions and to elaborate on the reasons for making selected predictions ("Why do you think so?").

2. Have students read to a predetermined logical stopping point in the text (this should be located by the teacher before students read). This point can be a major shift in the action of the story, the introduction of a new character, or the resolution of a story conflict.

3. Repeat the questions from step 1. Some of the predictions will be refined, some will be eliminated, and new ones will be formulated. Ask students, "How do you know?" to encourage clarification or verification. Redirect questions to several students (if working in a group situation).

4. Continue the reading to another logical stopping point. Continue to ask questions similar to those above.

5. Continue to the end of the text. Make sure the focus is on large units of text, rather than small sections, which tend to upset the flow of the narrative and disrupt adequate comprehension. As students move through the text, be sure to encourage thoughtful contemplation of the text, reflective discussion, and individual purposes for reading.

See page 230 for a sample lesson plan using this strategy.

▶ Asking Divergent Questions

Selected use of the following questions can help students appreciate the diversity of observations and responses they can make to literature. The intent is not to have students all arrive at "right answers," but rather to help them look at the diversity of thinking that they do while reading a piece of literature.

You may wish to post several of these questions on a chalkboard or sheet of paper duplicated for each student. Take a few moments to discuss some of these questions prior to having students read a book. Work with students to identify four to six questions that they may wish to be on the lookout for during the course of their reading. As appropriate, invite students to stop at one or two predetermined stopping points in the book. Take time at these junctures to talk about possible responses to selected questions. This allows students to see how others are interpreting a particular selection. However, the basic intent is to have students begin asking themselves these questions as they become more accomplished readers.

1. List all the words you can think of to describe _____.

2. What are all the possible solutions for _____?

3. List as many _____ as you can think of.

4. How would _____ view this?

5. What would _____ mean from the viewpoint of _____?

6. How would a _____ describe _____?

7. How would you feel if you were _____?

8. What would _____ do?

9. You are a _____. Describe your feelings.

10. How is _____ like _____?

11. I only know about _____. Explain _____ to me.

12. What ideas from _____ are like _____?

13. What _____ is most like a _____?

14. What would happen if there were more _____?

15. Suppose _____ happened, what would be the results?

16. Imagine if _____ and _____ were reversed. What would happen?

An Inside Look Prior to and during the reading of the book *Oceans* by Seymour Simon (New York: Morrow, 1990), fourth-grade teacher Robert Sanchez shares some of the following questions with a group of his students. As Robert states, "I was not my intent to force students into right or wrong answers. Rather, I wanted to help them think about what we were reading in the book, how it related to their own lives, and how selected facts could be looked at from a number of viewpoints." Here are some of Robert's queries:

• Make a list of all the words you can think of that describe an ocean.

• How would a seagull describe an ocean? How would a shark describe that same ocean?

• How would you feel if you were a piece of driftwood floating on the surface of the ocean?

• How are ocean currents like a river?

• You are a sea urchin. Describe your feelings about the rise and fall of tides.

• What do you think would happen if there was more salt in the oceans of the world?

• Suppose all the icebergs melted, what do you think might happen?

• Imagine that you had to live on a boat in the ocean for the next year. What habits would you need to change?

Robert's intent is to assist his students in becoming active thinkers during the reading of selected literature. While his initial focus is to present a small guided reading group with a book on oceanography, a secondary goal is to help the students use reading as a vehicle for learning in any area or endeavor. His use of divergent questions helps students process information instead of just committing it to memory. 📖

▶ MM & M (Metacognitive Modeling and Monitoring)

MM & M provides readers with an opportunity to "see" inside the mind of a reader as they go through the reading process. In essence you, the teacher, serve as a model of efficient reading—demonstrating for students the thought processes and mental activities used while reading. When struggling readers are made aware of the strategies readers use (inside their heads), they can emulate those strategies for themselves. MM & M gives students insight into the mind of an accomplished reader and demonstrates processes that can go on inside their heads as they read.

In this strategy you select a reading selection and begin to "think out loud," verbalizing what is going on inside your head as you read. Since students cannot observe the thinking process first-hand, the verbalization allows them to get a sense of good thinking as practiced by an accomplished reader. You serve as the most significant role model for students in all their academic endeavors, so your "talking while reading" gives them some firsthand experiences with reading as a thinking process, which they can begin to incorporate into their schema.

Initially, you will want to select a piece of textual material that is short and contains some obvious points of difficulty (vocabulary, sequence of events, ambiguities, etc.). Read the selected passage aloud to a guided reading group, stopping at selected points, and verbalizing the thought processes you are using to work through any difficulties. This verbalization is essential, because it provides a viable model for students to copy. Here are examples of the five steps:

1. Make predictions. (Demonstrate the importance of making hypotheses.)

"From this title, I predict that this story will be about a missing ring and a haunted house."

"In the next chapter, I think we'll find out how the two twins were able to sail to the other side of the lake."

"I think this next part will describe what the thief took from the dresser drawer."

2. Describe your mental images. (Show how mental pictures are formed in your head as you read.)

"I can see a picture of an old man walking down a country lane with his dog at his side."

"I'm getting a picture in my mind of a sparsely furnished apartment with very small rooms."

"The picture I have in my mind is that of a very short girl with curly red hair and a face full of freckles."

3. Share an analogy. (Show how the information in the text may be related to something in one's background knowledge.)

"This is like the time I had to take my daughter to the hospital in the middle of the night."

"This is similar to the time I first learned to ski in Colorado and kept falling down all the time."

"This seems to be like the day we had to take our family dog to the vet's to be put to sleep."

4. Verbalize a confusing point. (Show how you keep track of your level of comprehension as you read.)

"I'm not sure what is happening here."

"This is turning out a little differently than I expected."

"I guess I was correct in my original prediction."

5. Demonstrate "fix-up" strategies. (Let students see how you repair any comprehension problems.)

"I think I need to reread this part of the story."

"Maybe this word is explained later in the story."

"Now that part about the fishing rod makes sense to me."

These five steps can and should be modeled for students in several different kinds of reading material. As you read and model, allow students opportunities to interject their thoughts about what may be going on in their heads as they listen to the selection. Your goal, obviously, will be to have students internalize these processes and be able to do them on their own in all kinds of reading material. Here are some alternate approaches to MM & M:

Partner Pairs. Have students practice the procedure with a partner. One student reads a passage out loud to another and verbalizes some of the thinking taking place in his or her head as they read. The partner records those thought processes and discusses them with the reader upon completion of the story.

Hear This. Students can read a passage into a tape recorder. Afterward, a student can play the recording and stop at selected points and tell a partner or you about some of the thinking that was taking place in his or her head as he or she dealt with the text at that spot.

The More the Merrier. Bring in other adults to the classroom to model their thinking behavior as they read. The principal, secretary, custodian, librarian, superintendent, and other school-related personnel can all be held up to students as positive reading models. Be sure to provide a brief in-service on MM & M for each reader prior to his or her presentation.

Higher and Higher. Invite students from grades higher than yours to visit the classroom and read selected passages to your students. Ask them to model their thinking as they read.

Reader of the Day. Designate a student "Reader of the Day" who selects a passage to share with other students and demonstrates the MM & M procedure. This daily event designates every student as a model for all the other students and validates the utility of this strategy for all readers in all types of material.

An Inside Look   For more than 12 years Dara DePalma has been a fifth-grade teacher in Sunnyvale, California. She has been an ardent fan of guided reading ever since she attended an annual conference of the California Reading Association. While there, she had had an opportunity to hear several speakers discuss the dynamics of guided reading—dynamics Dara thought would re-energize her reading program.

One of the guided reading strategies Dara was most fascinated by was MM & M, which had been presented by the author of this book during the conference. After returning to her classroom the following week, Dara wanted to "test" this strategy with her students. She introduced one of her guided reading groups to the book *The River* by Gary Paulsen. Before students read the book, she demonstrated for them the following five stages:

1. **Make Predictions:** "From the title, I think that this story will be about a boy who takes a trip down a river and gets into some kind of danger."

2. **Describe Mental Images:** "As I close my eyes I can see a long river with lots of trees along the shore and a series of dangerous rapids downstream."

3. **Share an Analogy:** "This sounds like it might be similar to the time my husband and I rafted down part of the Colorado River four summers ago."

4. **Verbalize a Confusing Point** (after reading the first chapter aloud): "I'm not sure why this person wants Brian to go back into the woods again. I wonder what he is trying to get Brian to do."

5. **Demonstrate "Fix-up" Strategies:** "I think I'm going to need to read the next chapter or two in order to discover why this man wants Brian to repeat his experiences once again."

After the modeling process, Dara invited members of the group to duplicate each of the five stages for selected chapters of the book. After a few sessions, Dara noticed how involved students were in the text, and she observed increased levels of interest and comprehension. She also discovered new opportunities to discuss a book with her students, both before a book was read and at its conclusion. These discussions helped students understand their role in the reading process and the value of personal involvement (via a metacognitive strategy) in several different types of reading material .📖

▶ Metacognitive Questioning

Helping students begin asking their own self-initiated questions can be a powerful element in any guided reading session. In order to do that, students need models to emulate (as in the examples above). The goal of asking students appropriate metacognitive questions is to gradually release responsibility of question-asking and place it squarely in the hands of students.

The following chart will assist you in asking appropriate metacognitive questions in the During stage of a guided reading lesson. Teacher-posed questions are listed down the left side of the chart. The objective is to gradually reduce the amount of teacher questions and increase the number of student-posed questions—questions that students begin asking themselves as they read. You can post the list on the right for students or transcribe it onto individual index cards. You can distribute these cards randomly to a group of students and use them as discussion starters during or after the reading of an appropriate passage.

Teacher-Posed	Student-Posed
1. Is this story similar to anything you may have read before?	**1.** Why would this information be important for me to know?
2. What were you thinking when you read this part of the story?	**2.** Is this character similar to any other(s) I have read about?
3. What have we learned so far?	**3.** Does this information give me any clues as to what may happen later in the story?
4. What is the major point of this section?	**4.** How does this information differ from other things I know?
5. Did you change your mind about anything after reading this part of the story?	**5.** Why is this difficult for me to understand?
6. Do you have any personal questions about this book that have not been answered so far?	**6.** Do I need additional information to help me understand this topic?
7. What did you do when you didn't understand that word in the story?	**7.** Can I write a summary of this part of the story?
8. What makes you feel your interpretation is most appropriate?	**8.** What do I know so far?
9. What new information are you learning?	**9.** What did the author do to make me think this way?
10. How did you arrive at your interpretation?	**10.** Am I satisfied with this story?

▶ Self-Questioning

Providing students with opportunities to initiate their own questions throughout the reading process can be a valuable goal of guided reading instruction. Page 141 provides a list of questions accomplished and mature readers tend to ask themselves. Here is a modeling procedure you may wish to follow:

1. Select a piece of children's literature.

2. Ask yourself (out loud) some of the Before Reading questions, and provide answers for yourself (again, out loud).

3. Read the book aloud to a guided reading group.

4. Throughout the reading continue to ask yourself questions (this time from the During Reading list).

5. Complete the oral reading and once more ask yourself a sampling of questions from the After Reading section.

6. After several readings, ask a student to come forward and model similar processes for the group.

7. Invite other group members to demonstrate the steps outlined above.

8. Encourage students to select several questions from each of the three sections and respond to them in writing in their journals. After the reading of a piece of literature, use their questions and responses as discussion points in individual conferences.

An Inside Look Vickie Orwig loves Harry Potter. She loves to read Harry Potter books during her planning time, when she is relaxing at home, when she travels to visit her parents in Indiana, and especially during story sharing time in her classroom. As a sixth-grade teacher in Gainesville, Florida, Vickie has discovered the power of Harry Potter books in her classroom and in the lives of her students. Her sixth graders can't get enough of them and Vickie is just as enthralled with J. K. Rowlings's books as are her students.

As part of several selected guided reading lessons with her students, Vickie has duplicated and used the Self-Initiated Reading Queries form throughout the reading of the Harry Potter series. She believes that the form provides her students with "something to chew on" as they pore through the books. Just as important is the fact that the form offers numerous opportunities for students within a group to share and discuss their interpretations.

As part of a session with a guided reading group who was reading the fourth book in the series—*Harry Potter and The Goblet of*

Fire—Vickie invited students to complete the Before Reading section of the form. During the follow-up discussion, Vickie discovered a wide range of interpretations and discovery questions within the group. Discussion was instantaneous as a result. The completion of the During Reading and After Reading sections also produced a non-stop flow of queries and conversation that seemed to have no end.

While Vickie does not use the form for every book and every guided reading session, she has found it to be a marvelous tool for stimulating and encouraging quality conversation. She has also been able to focus on the development of specific comprehension skills with selected students.

▶ Cooperative Learning

One of the ways students can be supported in their literature adventures is through cooperative learning. Following are some brief examples of cooperative learning methods. It is important to note how these methods can become integral elements of guided reading lessons. Indeed, when students have opportunities to learn from each other in the pursuit of mutual goals, the vitality and purpose of guided reading is enhanced and strengthened.

1. Jigsaw. Assign students to various guided reading groups to work on material that you have divided into sections. Team members read and study their respective sections. Next, members of different teams who have studied the same material meet in "expert groups" to share their findings. Then the students return to their team and teach their teammates about the information.

2. Web Weavers. Assign three or four students to a guided reading group prior to reading a story. Give a large piece of poster paper or chart-pack paper to the group. Provide each member of the group with a different color pen or felt-tipped marker. Draw a preliminary semantic web for the story on the paper. Each student (in turn) then records his or her background knowledge or prior experiences around the categories designated on the web. Students discuss any similarities and/or differences. As the read the story, students record new data on the web.

3. Prediction People. Organize students into groups of three or four and provide each group with a prediction "map" (a large sheet of paper). Encourage each member of the group to write a prediction (for a forthcoming story) on the map and discuss his or her reasons for recording that information. The group talks and arrives at a common prediction. As they read the story, students stop at selected spots and change, modify, or rewrite their initial predictions. The group's prediction is also changed, modified, or rewritten.

4. Reader's Roundtable. Assign the members of a guided reading group the same book. The group is responsible for dividing the reading into several parts (as in "readers theater") and assigning readings to individual members. Afterward, each group member shares her or his interpretation with other members of the group. Allow time to discuss any differences in interpretation with individual members.

An Inside Look Jaime Velasquez, a recent graduate of the University of Arizona, has recently secured a teaching position in San Diego, California. Assigned to fourth grade, he knows that he will have a wide diversity of students in his classroom—a host of languages, a variety of reading levels, and a range of interests, needs, and abilities. From some of his methods courses in college, he knows that guided reading can provide him with important teaching opportunities that can assist each of his students in achieving significant levels of reading comprehension. He also knows that guided reading is but one element in his overall reading curriculum.

At the start of the school year, Jamie introduces his students to a combination unit on animals. His intent is to integrate his reading program into content area subjects, such as science. Jamie determines the various levels of reading ability in his class through the assessment tests presented earlier in this book. He then assigns each of the groups the book *Amazing Animals* by Anthony D. Fredericks and Sneed Collard (Minnetonka, MN: NorthWord Press, 2000). This book is a compilation of stories and descriptions of 60 different and unusual animals from around the world. Jamie gives each group a large sheet of paper on which he has drawn the web at the left:

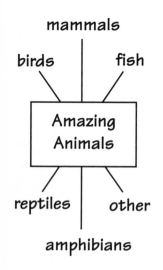

Jamie gives each student a different color of marker and asks each to write examples of animals for each of the identified categories. Each group then discusses the animals they have listed and the "appropriateness" of those animals for each category. Jamie encourages students to look for additional animals during their reading that can be added to the web.

Jamie has found that the cooperative learning strategy of Web Weavers provides him with a way to access students' background knowledge as well as a method to help shape their comprehension of a text in several different ways. 📖

▶ Sequence Chain

The Sequence Chain provides students with an opportunity to create a graphic representation of the events in a story as they happen. It is appropriate for students to use this device as they are reading the story or immediately upon its conclusion.

Make sufficient copies of the diagram on page 142 for each student in the group. Invite each student as he or she reads the story to record a significant story event in each separate box (additional boxes may be added; empty boxes may be eliminated).

After each student has had an opportunity to record selected events within this diagram, invite her or him to go back into the story to validate each of the events or selected events. This offers students opportunities to confirm their original information and build a positive link between the information in the story and that recorded on the diagrams.

▶ Setting Spider Web

This web offers several options for you and your students (see page 143 for a sample blank web). Its intent is to help students focus on the elements, features, and conditions that contribute to the setting of a story. Students need to know that story setting is related both to the *place* in which a story happens as well as the *time* in which it takes place. Select one of the following designs and share it with the students.

• Write the setting of the story in the circle in the middle of each web. Duplicate the web and provide a copy for each student. Invite students, as they each read the story to themselves, to look

for words or phrases that relate to or are linked with the setting. Each word can be written on a "spoke" of the web. After the story is completed, invite students to compare and contrast their various webs.

• Write selected setting "clues" on several of the spokes of the web. Duplicate the diagram and provide a copy for each student. Invite students to look for additional clues as they read the story and record those on their individual copies. After they've read the story, allow time for students to discuss their similarities and differences.

• Provide copies of a blank setting web to each student. As students read, invite them to record a "clue" on a selected spoke. Then each student can pass the web to the next student in the circle. Repeat the process several times. At the conclusion of the story invite students to look at all the collective "clues" and decide on an appropriate term or phrase to place in the center of each web.

• Write the word *Time* in the center circle of the web. Make sufficient copies of the web for each student in a group. Invite students to read a selected story and, as they read, to write any "time" words (such as *before, after, soon,* or *once*) on the spokes around the web. Plan time afterward to discuss all the words and clues that indicate time elements in the story.

An Inside Look Mark Jarmel has been using both the Sequence Chain and the Setting Spider Web with his fourth-grade students in Allentown, Pennsylvania, for nearly 15 years. He has discovered that the use of these two graphic organizers has provided his students with a visual reminder of the information they learn while reading as well as its relationship to their individual and collective background knowledge.

Mark uses both of these techniques primarily with fiction material since it offers young readers some insights into two very important components of narrative material. By inviting his students to record necessary data in each of these two structures, Mark can assess how well students are focusing on important information and whether they can understand the relevance of isolated details to each other. This data encourages conversation with a guided reading group and also provides a vehicle for individual conferences between Mark and selected students. This results in active discourse between and among guided reading group members—one of the primary objectives in Mark's reading program. 📖

▶ Feelings Web

The Feelings Web provides students with an opportunity to chart and measure the changes that take place in a major character during the course of a story. The quality of a piece of literature is often determined by the changes a character makes during the course of a story. The character's personality is established early in the story, a problem or conflict is presented, the character must use her or his special qualities to solve the problems, there is some resolution of the problem, and the character is changed in some way.

The Feelings Web provides students with an opportunity to chart the feelings a character goes through during an extended story. It also provides an important vehicle for guided reading group discussions. Several teachers ask selected students to complete these webs over the course of a day or week and then explain those changes to their classmates. Such a process helps make a positive link between the emotions of students in the class and the emotions of characters in a book.

A blank Feelings Web appears on page 143. See page 217 for a sample lesson plan using this strategy.

▶ Character Map

The Character Map helps students understand how the events of a story contribute to the personality of a major character. Each student in a guided reading group may select separate characters or they may each select the same character. During the reading of the book, students write selected events in the boxes around the perimeter of the web. Students can determine (individually or in small groups) the character trait that is depicted by the events and the character's reaction to those events. Upon completion of the book, the teacher encourages students to discuss and modify their perceptions in light of the reactions of other members of the group.

A blank Character Map appears on page 145.

An Inside Look To most tourists driving through Hilo, Hawaii, on their way to Hawaii Volcanoes National Park, the town looks like a sleepy village anchoring the northeastern edge of the big island of Hawaii. But don't tell that to Farrah Hallisey and her third-grade students. Their classroom is a hotbed of activity and a seething cauldron of excitement and enthusiasm. Farrah infuses her class-room with a plethora of books representing all genres and all interest levels of her students. Each and every subject she teaches is supple-mented by quality literature, both fiction and nonfiction. To say that Farrah's classroom was a miniature library within a school would be to state the obvious. Books spill over the counters, fall from the shelves, and lay scattered across every desk, table, and horizontal surface in the room.

Farrah uses Character Maps with several different types of lit-erature. A strong believer in the value of guided reading as part of an overall literacy program, she seeks to engage her students in a vari-ety of personal and active learning experiences. Character Maps pro-vide her students with graphic organizers that focus on the qualities and features of selected individuals with narrative writing. By focus-ing on the traits and events that help shape a book character's per-sonality, Farrah helps students develop appropriate models that they can use in their own writing. So, too, can her students begin to under-stand the relationships that can and do exist between book characters and people in their own lives. This assists them in developing well-rounded characters for their own writing episodes. 📖

▶ Five Circles

This graphic organizer encourages students to focus on a single char-acter, a problem that character has, a possible solution for the prob-lem, and how that individual eventually solves the problem. Students are provided with opportunities to make sincere and authentic predictions based upon information they are reading in the book in concert with their own backgrounds of experience. This graphic organizer allows several members of a guided reading group to each focus on a selected character and combine their perceptions into an overall picture of how various characters deal with selected issues.

A blank Five Circles diagram appears on page 146. See page 213 for a sample lesson plan using this strategy.

▶ Details + Main Idea

This graphic organizer encourages students (either individually or in a small group setting) to isolate individual details in a story. Prior instruction is centered on assisting students in isolating important from non-important details. When students are comfortable in capturing significant and important details (to be recorded in the rectangles above the line) invite them to create an appropriate main idea that is representative of this collection of facts. *Note:* It is not necessary for students to fill in every one of the "detail" boxes.

You may wish to walk students through the process using a recently completed book or chapter in the basal text. A blank Details + Main Idea diagram appears on page 147.

An Inside Look When Amanda Killion was first introduced to the Details + Main Idea strategy, she knew it would be a wonderful addition to her reading curriculum. As a fifth-grade teacher in a small school district outside of Birmingham, Alabama, she wants her students to understand the various relationships that help to build a well-crafted story. Whenever she reads a new book aloud to her students, she models how to fill in the blanks on an oversized Details + Main Idea chart that she has posted in the front of the classroom. She duplicated and enlarged the chart from this book. Amanda took the enlarged version to a local office supply store and had it laminated. She then affixed it to the top of the chalkboard.

As she reads, Amanda stops every so often to fill in a significant detail on the chart (using a wipe-off marker). She explains to her students reasons why she has selected each detail and why that detail is important to an overall comprehension of the story. Upon concluding the story, she engages students in a discussion about how those details add up to a single main idea. Students discuss several possibilities and then write their main ideas on the chart.

When Amanda organizes students into guided reading groups, she reminds them of the process they went through with the Details + Main Idea chart as a whole class. She then encourages students to go through the same process on individual copies of the chart. The result is lots of discussion and lots of give and take within any single group. 📖

▶ Cause/Effect

This graphic organizer encourages students to look at how certain events in a story are precipitated by other events or how events can shape the outcome of a story. Duplicate several copies of this form and provide a sheet for each member of a guided reading group. As students are reading a book or story, invite them to list various outcomes in the Effect boxes (for example, a character runs away, a house is flooded, a dog is found, or a villain is defeated). Then invite students to go back in the story to determine the story details that caused each event to occur. This would be an ideal time for students to engage in a variety of cooperative learning strategies in order to arrive at mutually satisfying responses. Plan adequate time for students to discuss their selections as well as to defend their choices. *Note:* Depending on the length or complexity of the story selected, you may need to add additional Cause/Effect boxes.

A blank Cause/Effect diagram appears on page 148.

▶ Opinion/Fact

This graphic organizer can be utilized in a variety of ways. Here are a few suggestions:

1. Provide each member of a guided reading group with a copy of the Opinion/Fact diagram. Invite each student to search for three critical facts in a story. These facts can be filled in the three Fact boxes. At the end of the story, ask each student to record her or his personal opinion about those facts (to be recorded in the Opinion box). Provide opportunities for group members to share and discuss any similarities and/or differences.

2. Give a guided reading group a single copy of the blank form. Encourage group members to work together to fill in three (and only three) significant details from the story. After sufficient discussion, ask the group to arrive at a single and all-encompassing opinion about the facts collectively or the story as a whole.

3. Provide each member of a guided reading group with an individual copy of the Opinion/Fact diagram. Assign the "setting" of the story to one student, the "main character" to another student, and specific "events" (determined by you beforehand) to other students. Invite each child to complete her or his form. Afterward, encourage youngsters to discuss the information they recorded to determine any relationships.

A blank Opinion/Fact diagram appears on page 149.

An Inside Look Chrissy Rodriguez has been using graphic organizers with her fifth-grade students in Santa Fe, New Mexico, for many years. As part of her graduate work in reading, she and several other local teachers developed a series of graphic organizers that could be used with a wide range of reading materials. This group of upper elementary teachers wanted to take some of the techniques and strategies that had been used so successfully by their primary-level colleagues and adapt them to the books and literature shared with upper elementary students.

Two graphic organizers that Chrissy is particularly fond of include the Cause/Effect and the Opinion/Fact plans. Chrissy has discovered that these two techniques provide her students with opportunities to investigate and compare selected elements of narrative writing in a cooperative atmosphere. As an example, Crissy loves to have her students read the *Skinneybones* series by Barbara Park. Children have enjoyed the humor and well-crafted characters for years and the books never fail to excite Crissy's students. She has read them aloud to her class and used them in a variety of guided reading lessons.

One of the techniques Crissy uses is to provide a guided reading group with a copy of the Opinion/Fact chart and invite students to individually complete the form with various facts about Alex (the main character). Afterward, students engage in conversation comparing and contrasting their factual information. The group then works together to arrive at a mutually agreeable opinion about Alex. The spirited discussion is an opportunity to share the elements of good characterization (for which Barbara Park is known) as well as how a character can drive the plot of a story.

▶ Mountain Diagram

The Mountain Diagram provides a graphic organizer through which students can focus on the essential events of a story. It helps them recognize the events that lead up to the story climax and those circumstances that follow a climactic event.

Students in a guided reading group work together to list the pre-climax events along the left side of the "mountain." Then they list the climax of the story or book at the top of the "mountain." Events that follow the climax are placed on the lines going down the right side of the "mountain." Students then have an opportunity to decide on the story theme(s) for the reading material and fill in the appropriate box in the center of the diagram.

A blank Mountain Diagram appears on page 150. See page 257 for a sample lesson plan using this strategy.

Name _____   **Date** _____

Book _____

Self-Initiated Reading Queries

Pre-reading
_____ Is this similar to anything I have read before?
_____ Why am I reading this?
_____ Why would this information be important for me to know?
_____ Do I have any questions about the text before I read it?
If so, what are they?

During Reading
_____ Am I understanding what I'm reading?
_____ What can I do if I don't understand this information?
_____ Why am I learning this?
_____ Are these characters or events similar to others I have read?
_____ How does this information differ from other things that I know?
_____ Why is this difficult or easy for me to understand?
_____ Is this interesting or enjoyable? Why or why not?
_____ Do I have any questions about this text that have not been answered so far?
_____ What new information am I learning?
_____ What information do I still need to learn?

After Reading
_____ Can I write a brief summary of the story?
_____ What did I learn in this story?
_____ Where can I go to learn some additional information on this topic?
_____ Did I confirm (or do I need to modify) my initial purpose for reading this text?
_____ Is there anything else interesting I'd like to find out about this topic?
_____ Do I have some unanswered questions from this text?

Name _____ Date _____

Book _____

Sequence Chain

Name _____ **Date** _____

Book _____

Setting Spider Web

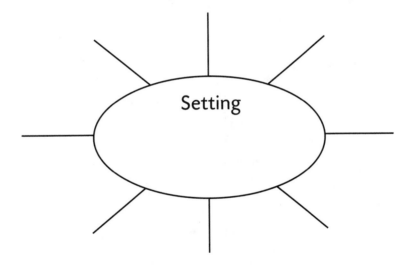

Name _____ **Date** _____

Book _____

Feelings Web

```
┌─────────────────────┐                    ┌─────────────────────┐
│ When?               │                    │ When?               │
│                     │                    │                     │
│ Why?                │                    │ Why?                │
│                     │                    │                     │
└─────────────────────┘                    └─────────────────────┘
```

(Feeling)   *(Feeling)*

```
            ┌─────────────────────────┐
            │   Name of Character     │
            └─────────────────────────┘
```

(Feeling)   *(Feeling)*

```
┌─────────────────────┐                    ┌─────────────────────┐
│ When?               │                    │ When?               │
│                     │                    │                     │
│ Why?                │                    │ Why?                │
│                     │                    │                     │
└─────────────────────┘                    └─────────────────────┘
```

Name _____ **Date** _____

Book _____

Character Map

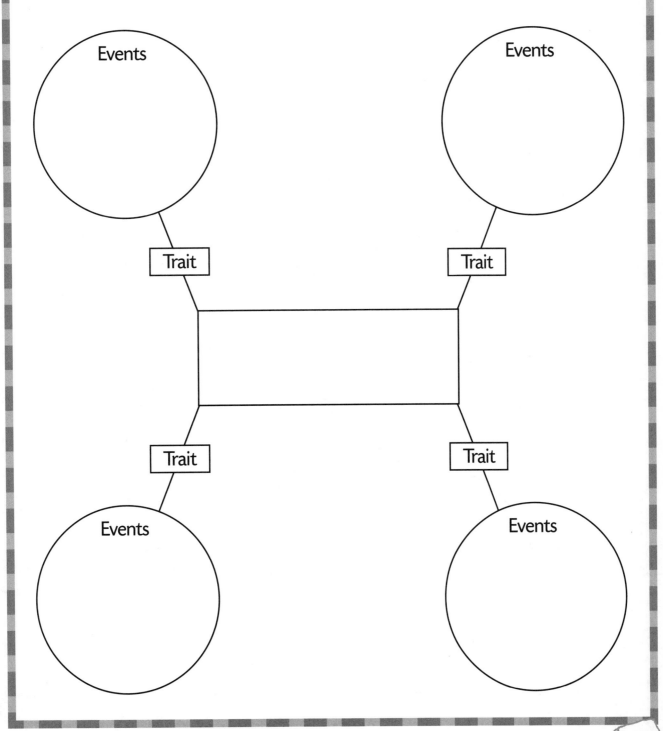

Name _____ **Date** _____

Book _____

Five Circles

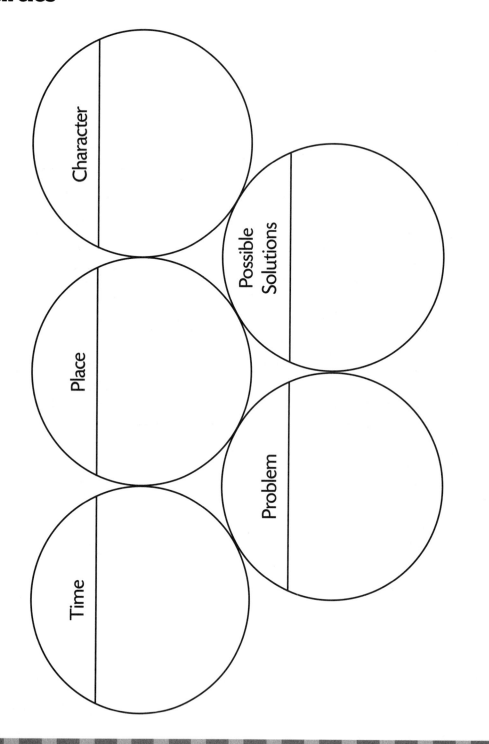

Name _____ **Date** _____

Book _____

Details + Main Idea

Details

+

Main Idea

Name _____ **Date** _____

Book _____

Cause/Effect Chart

Cause	Effect

Name _____   **Date** _____

Book _____

Opinion and Fact Chart

Opinion:

Fact:		Fact:

Fact:

Name _____ **Date** _____

Book _____

Mountain Diagram

Climax: _____

_____

_____

_____

_____

Story themes:

Events leading to climax

Events following climax

After Reading Strategies

Reading strategies that are shared with students after reading a book serve to enrich and extend students' learning. The following strategies encourage students to transfer what they have read to real-life situations. Additionally, judicious use of these suggestions will enable readers to apply what they have learned in a variety of texts. These ideas also help students build bridges to new learning opportunities. These strategies are particularly effective in a host of guided reading lesson plans.

▶ Continuums

Character Continuum. The Character Continuum is a delightful post-reading strategy that helps students discuss information related to the qualities and characteristics of selected characters in a story. With some minor modifications, this strategy can also be used to help students focus on the setting in a story.

1. Ask students to brainstorm all of the words they can think of that can be used to describe one or more characters in a story. Write the words on the chalkboard or overhead projector.

2. Invite students to suggest antonyms for most or all of the recorded words.

3. Place each word pair at opposite ends of a continuum (see page 152). For intermediate students 8 to 12 lines are adequate.

4. Invite students to work in pairs or as a whole group to place an X on each line indicating the degree to which an identified character exhibits a particular trait (there are no right or wrong answers).

5. Encourage students to discuss their rationale for placement of the Xs. Rereading of portions of the book may be necessary to verify information or assumptions.

6. Students may wish to create a Master Continuum, which can be duplicated and used repeatedly with other characters in other stories.

A blank Character Continuum appears on page 172.

Setting Continuum. Page 173 is an example of a Setting Continuum that can be used with students. The words and their antonyms have all been suggested by third-grade guided reading groups. Invite your students to suggest their own words (and their opposites) for continuums used in your classroom.

Facts/Attitude Continuum. Page 174 shows a Facts/Attitude Continuum, which is appropriate for use with nonfiction material. The procedure is similar to that outlined above, except that students are encouraged to suggest facts about a topic as well as their attitudes or perceptions of that topic, too. These items (and their accompanying antonyms) are arranged on continuum lines as the strategy discussed above. Students are invited to complete these after reading a book. Note: This is also appropriate as a pre-reading strategy with students suggesting ideas based on their background knowledge of a forthcoming topic.

An Inside Look Ward Kessler's third-grade students created the following Character Continuum for the book *The Island-Below-the-Star* by James Rumford (Boston: Houghton Mifflin, 1998). This is an engaging story about five brothers, including one named Manu, each with a special skill, who set sail across the vast Pacific Ocean to the islands now known as Hawaii. The following continuum was created after students in one guided reading group had read the first part of the book to the class.

Sample Character Continuum

Book Title: ___The Island–Below–the–Star___

Character: ___Manu___

Friendly.X...Unfriendly

Happy.X...Sad

Popular......................X............Unpopular

Wise...............................X.........Foolish

Outgoing...................X...................Shy

Unselfish..................X...............Selfish

Sociable.................................X......Unsociable

```
Ambitious......X...............................Lazy
Neat.......................X.........................Messy
Honest..........................................X.....Dishonest
Brave............X.................................Cowardly
Kind...X.............................................Cruel
```

After students had completed the Character Continuum, they each read the rest of the book silently. Ward then invited students to consider repositioning any of their Xs on the Continuum as a result of reading the second half of the story. In this way, Ward helped his students understand that characters change, grow, and develop throughout a story. 📖

▶ Plot Graph

The Plot Graph allows students to design a graphic representation of the plot of a story. In so doing, they are able to use selected math skills in concert with a pictorial display of the sequence of events in a story or book. This post-reading strategy is particularly useful in helping students understand the utility of charts and graphs in realistic situations as well as to comprehend the "flow" of a story from beginning to end. To use this strategy:

1. Provide students with graph paper and invite them to select four or five of the major events of a story to record (in sequence) at the bottom of the sheet.

2. Encourage students to record numbers up the left-hand side of the graph indicating degrees of intensity.

3. After students have finished reading a story, invite them to plot each of the selected events on the graph according to their own perceptions of intensity (see page 155).

4. Students may wish to use their Plot Graphs as an aid to journal writing or summarization activities.

A blank Plot Graph form appears on page 175. See page 236 for a sample lesson plan using this strategy.

An Inside Look Throughout her 18 years of teaching third grade in Logan, Utah, Verna Cannon has been a fan of Eve Bunting. She has collected every book Eve Bunting has written, she has assembled a collection of Eve Bunting lesson plans that span the curriculum, and she has developed an Eve Bunting thematic unit that she uses every spring. Bookshelves are filled with Eve Bunting books and read-aloud sessions are sure to include a healthy dose of Eve Bunting books.

Verna likes Eve Bunting as an author because of her simple, direct way of touching the lives of readers through realistic stories filled with plausible characters and current events. Verna was ecstatic when Eve Bunting's book *Smoky Night* was presented with the Caldecott Medal in 1995. She quickly developed a new series of lessons revolving around that single book.

One of the strategies Verna includes in her lessons is the Plot Graph. She knows that this strategy enables her students to see how an accomplished writer develops a story from beginning to end. Verna also knows that Plot Graphing provides her young writers with a positive model to emulate.

Following is an example of a plot graph that Verna and one of her guided reading groups developed for the book *Smoky Night*. It details significant events and how they are connected. Additionally, it illustrates how a plot develops, how it builds to a climax, and how it concludes. You can use this format (along with the description of the technique above) as a model for your own Plot Graphs. This particular technique has many uses in many different types of narrative literature.

Book Title: _____ Smoky Night _____

Author: _____ Eve Bunting _____

Character: _____ Daniel _____

Personality Characteristic: _____ Fear _____

| | Watch riots | Lose cat | Go to shelter | Find cat |

Summary: Daniel and his mother are caught up in the Los Angeles riots, something Daniel doesn't fully understand. During the rioting, Daniel's cat is lost. He and his mother are shepherded to a local shelter, where they meet many interesting people. Daniel is finally reunited with his cat.

▶ Story Pyramid

The Story Pyramid (Waldo, 1991) helps students focus on main characters, important settings, and the problem/solution of a selected piece of literature. It can be used with individual readers in a guided reading group or may be presented as a group activity. The Story Pyramid invites students to complete a triangular outline of story elements using the following information:

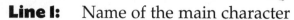

Line 1: Name of the main character
Line 2: Two words describing the main character
Line 3: Three words describing the setting
Line 4: Four words stating the problem
Line 5: Five words describing the main event
Line 6: Six words describing a second main event
Line 7: Seven words describing a third main event
Line 8: Eight words stating the solution to the problem

A blank Story Pyramid form appears on page 176.

An Inside Look Becky Oliver, a fifth-grade teacher in Wichita, Kansas, has always enjoyed sharing the book *Hatchet* by Gary Paulsen with her students. As part of a guided reading lesson, she invites one of the high fifth-grade groups to read the book and complete (on an individual basis) a story pyramid. One of her students, Dudley, completes the pyramid as follows:

1. Brian
2. Brave resourceful
3. Wilderness lake forest
4. Survive on his own
5. Pilot suffers a heart attack
6. Brian starts a fire by himself
7. Brian swims out to plane and explores
8. Brian is rescued by a pilot flying nearby

Becky asks each of the members of the group to share their individual Story Pyramids with one another. A healthy discussion ensues as students defend their choice of events and descriptive words with each other.

▶ Literature Log

A Literature Log provides students with opportunities to think about what they have read and to organize that information into a systematic piece of writing. These should not be interpreted as "worksheets" since there are no right or wrong answers to any literature log. They can be used by individuals or small groups of students as a way to record information and thoughts about a particular book. As such, you may find them important to use as assessment tools or as summary sheets to be maintained in each student's portfolio.

The first Literature Log on page 177 is appropriate for use at the conclusion of a book or story. The Log on page 178 can be used by students prior to, during, and after the reading of a book. See page 239 for a sample lesson plan using this strategy.

▶ Answer First!

Answer First! is a questioning strategy that encourages and stimulates thinking at higher levels of comprehension. It allows you to direct students to more sophisticated levels of comprehension through the careful and judicious sequencing of questioning skills. This strategy has proven to be quite successful with all types of readers and is a particularly worthwhile addition to the work of any guided reading group. In fact, it can be used as either an individual activity or a small-group activity with equal results.

In Answer First!, you invite a guided reading group to read a selected book or text. Before reading, design a series of answers without questions, which you give to students on sheets of paper. The task of students, upon completion of the book, is to formulate questions, based on the material they read, that will generate the answers on the Answer First! sheet.

See page 244 for a sample lesson plan using this strategy.

An Inside Look The following fictitious story was created by Marjorie Whisken, a third-grade teacher in St. Paul, Minnesota. Marjorie wanted to introduce her students to the Answer First! strategy through a story she wrote so that they would not be influenced by a book or author they may have read previously. After students were comfortable with this strategy, Marjorie planned to present it to guided reading groups as part of their discussion and interpretation of selected books. She prepared the answers that follow the selection ahead of time and gave them to students after they read the passage. Marjorie gave them the responsibility for creating appropriate questions for each answer. She encouraged students to share and discuss possible questions in their groups before deciding on an appropriate question for each designated response.

Turtle Time

Most people don't think about turtles very often—yet, they are some of nature's most amazing creatures. Consider the fact that some tortoises (a terrestrial turtle) have been known to live well past their 200th birthday; and there have been a few who have lived more than 300 years! Another amazing fact about turtles and tortoises is their weight. There are many species that weigh well over 500 pounds (about as much as seven fifth-grade students in the same place at the same time). The leatherneck turtle, which spends most of its time in the ocean, frequently weighs in at 1,000 pounds or more. A long life and enormous body weight seem to be hallmarks of these remarkable and incredible creatures.

Another interesting fact about turtles is that they will often hibernate during the winter months (depending on the species). Some species of turtles will burrow into the sand or mud, slow down their body functions—including heart rate and breathing—and "sleep" their way through the winter. During this time the turtle seldom moves and is able to keep its body just warm enough to survive. Since turtles are cold-blooded animals, their body temperatures are the same as the surroundings in which they live.

Undoubtedly, the characteristics turtles and tortoises are most noted for is their extreme slowness. Many are very slow-moving land animals, although several species of sea turtles can move quite rapidly through the water. Both the turtle's heart rate and respiration rate are quite slow, as is its eating habits, which are pedestrian by human standards. Even their eggs can take a year or more to hatch! It seems as though most turtles and tortoises are quite content to go through life at a severely reduced pace.

Question:_____

  Answer: It is a turtle that lives on land._____

Question:_____

  Answer: So that they can conserve energy._____

Question:_____

  Answer: It may be due to their low heart and respiration rate.

Question: _____

Answer: <u>It must eat a large amount of food each day.</u>

Question: _____

Answer: <u>Take it easy!</u>

Note that in the example above the answers previously determined by Marjorie begin at the literal level of cognition and progressively move students to higher levels of cognition (comprehension, application, analysis, synthesis, evaluation) in a systematic way. This is the major advantage of this guided reading strategy—students can begin to read and interpret various forms of reading material at increased levels of understanding. Marjorie and many other teachers have successfully used Answer First! with both fiction and nonfiction materials and across a wide range of student abilities. What often results is that students can then generate their own questions at higher levels of cognition, too.

▶ Cloze Technique

In the Cloze technique, you prepare sentences or paragraphs in which selected words have been omitted. For example, you may wish to delete every fifth or every tenth word, or you may wish to delete all the nouns or all the adjectives from a chapter in a book. When you have decided on the words to be deleted from the piece, retype it, leaving blank spaces for the deleted words (it is suggested that each blank be the same length so that students cannot infer words based solely on their length). The retyped piece can then be used with students as part of a guided reading lesson. The advantage of Cloze is that it allows you to focus on specific grammatical concepts within the context of a familiar and contextually appropriate piece of writing. Students are then encouraged to work together or by themselves to replace the missing words with words that "sound right" or that make sense in the selection.

An Inside Look Following is a Cloze piece developed by Erica Hammond for her fifth-grade students. She took a portion of text from the book *Clever Camouflagers* by Anthony D. Fredericks (Minnetonka, MN: NorthWord Press, 1997) and retyped it onto a sheet of acetate for use on the overhead projector. As she prepared

the piece, she deleted selected nouns and replaced each one with a blank of ten spaces. She then projected the story sample on the screen and invited students in one guided reading group to contribute nouns that would help restore a sense of meaning to the original story (Erica was not interested in having students replicate the exact words she had deleted from the text, but rather wanted them to focus on a specific part of speech within a familiar book).

Scientists tell us that the colors and shapes of _____ have come about (or evolved) over thousands or _____ of years. An _____ is able to survive because it has adapted to its _____ — it knows how to locate its _____ and what to do to hide from its _____ . To do that, some _____ have developed distinctive means of _____ , pretending to be something they are not. 📖

▶ Story Frames

A Story Frame (Fowler, 1982) is a basic outline of a story that is designed to help the reader or writer organize his or her thoughts about a story. A "frame" consists of a series of extended blanks (similar in nature to the Cloze procedure), which are linked together by transition words or phrases. Story Frames differ from the Cloze in that students are provided longer blanks to complete and are given more latitude in selecting appropriate words or phrases. Following is a Story Frame that could be used in helping students focus on a particular character in a story.

This story is about_____

_____ ,

who is an important character. _____

tried to _____

_____

_____

_____

_____ .

The story ends when _____

_____ .

When completed, story frames can serve as discussion starters for the components of good stories as well as an outline for students who need a support structure for the creation of their own stories. Obviously, the intent is not to have all students arrive at an identical story, but rather to provide them with the freedom they need to create stories within appropriate grammatical contexts. Examples on pages 180–82 offer additional story frames you may find appropriate for your classroom. See pages 223 and 252 for sample lesson plans using this strategy.

▶ Readers Theatre

Readers Theatre is a storytelling device that stimulates the imagination and promotes *all* of the language arts. Simply stated, it is an oral interpretation of a piece of literature read in a dramatic style. However, its value goes far beyond that simple definition. It is an act of involvement, an opportunity to share, a time to creatively interact with others, and a personal interpretation of what can be or could be. Readers Theatre holds the promise of helping students in a guided reading group understand and appreciate the richness of language, the ways in which to interpret that language, and how language can be a powerful vehicle for the comprehension and appreciation of different forms of literature.

Consider some of the following in producing and presenting Readers Theatre scripts:

Much of the setting for a story should take place in the audience's mind.

Usually, all of the characters will be on stage throughout the duration of the presentation.

Most presentations will have a narrator to set up the story.

Each "actor" should have his or her own copy of the script.

The readers should have an opportunity to practice their script before presenting it to an audience.

The characters should focus on the audience rather than on each other.

Students should not memorize their lines, but rather should rehearse them sufficiently so that they are "comfortable" with them.

Presenting a Readers Theatre script need not be an elaborate or extensive production. As students become more familiar and polished

in using Readers Theatre, they will be able to suggest a multitude of presentation possibilities. Initially, students may be unfamiliar with the format of Readers Theatre. It would be important to discuss with students the fact that Readers Theatre is very similar to movie and television scripts and are written in much the same way. As in Hollywood, the intent is to take a basic story and turn it into a play or movie. With your students, discuss the original stories used as the foundation of these scripts and the resultant Readers Theatre scripts.

Lead your students in a whole-class activity to model the steps used in designing a Readers Theatre script. You'll need a sheet of chart-pack paper, a large piece of posterboard, or the overhead projector. Using a familiar story, begin to rewrite so that the entire class can see the steps. These steps might include:

- Rewriting the title to give it a more humorous slant
- Eliminating unnecessary dialogue or minor characters
- Inserting a Narrator at strategic points to advance the action or identify specific scenes
- Adding words that describe the tone of voice used by a specific character (such as *rapidly, irritated,* or *confused*)
- Underlining or bold-facing the names of characters for easy identification
- Creating new dialogue, characters, or settings to advance the story
- Consideration of the props necessary for the story

There is no ideal series of steps to follow in the design of Readers Theatre scripts. It is important, however, that students have some models to follow so that they will be encouraged and supported in the creation of their own scripts. Encourage students to work together to design their Readers Theatre scripts. It would be advantageous to appoint one student within a guided reading group to serve as the Scribe or Reporter. Each Recorder should understand that writing goes through many stages, so the first couple of ideas are just that—initial thoughts that can be eliminated or expanded according to the wishes and desires of the group.

Following is an example of a Readers Theatre script that could be used after a guided reading group has read one or more of Grimm's fairy tales. See page 227 for another Readers Theatre script example.

Don't Kiss Sleeping Beauty, She's Got Really Bad Breath

Staging: The narrator stands off to the side. The characters can each sit on a separate stool or chair. They may wish to stand in a circle in front of the audience, too.

Narrator

X

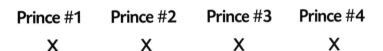

Prince #1   Prince #2   Prince #3   Prince #4

X   X   X   X

Narrator: Now here's another story that also happened a long time ago. I guess that's just the way it is with fairy tales, they all seemed to have taken place in the "good old days"—you know, the days before microwave ovens and cellular telephones. Anyway, once upon a time, there was this incredibly beautiful princess who was so good-looking that all the princes from miles around wanted to marry her. Every time she walked down the street, all the princes would stand around with their tongues hanging out of their mouths just hoping to get a look at her. She was one gorgeous lady. Now, in order to make this story somewhat interesting, we have to have an evil character, and, as is usually the case, the evil character in this and other stories just happens to be a wicked witch (gee, it sure does seem like there's an awful lot of wicked witches running around fairy tales, doesn't it?). In this story, the wicked witch gets the incredibly beautiful princess to eat some kind of semi-poisoned food and the princess immediately falls into a deep sleep. The witch makes the mistake of tossing the poison bottle in the town garbage dump. One of the princes finds it and notices that the antidote to the poison is a kiss from a handsome prince.

Prince #1: Wow! All I have to do is kiss Sleeping Beauty and she will awaken from her sleep to be my bride.

Narrator: (to the prince) That's right, Prince #1.

Narrator: (to the audience) Obviously, this guy isn't playing with a full deck. But anyway, let's jump ahead to when Prince #1 returns to the castle to tell his prince friends about his adventures.

Prince #1: Hey, guys. You're not going to believe this, but that Sleeping Beauty woman is sound asleep in that small cottage at the edge of the enchanted forest, just waiting for one of us to stop by and give her a kiss that will wake her up.

Prince #2: Well, why didn't you kiss her?

Prince #1: Well, it seems as though our fair maiden has bad breath. . . . I mean really bad breath! It was so bad that all the flowers in the house had wilted and the wallpaper was peeling off the walls. WHEW! Boy, did it stink!

Prince #3: You mean, you didn't kiss her after all?

Prince #1: No way, José. I couldn't even get in the room. I mean, even the flies were dropping like flies!

Prince #4: That's unbelievable. Here's this incredibly gorgeous princess, sleeping like a baby in the cottage just down the road, and we can't even get close enough to kiss her. Wow, what a waste!

Prince #1: Yea, and just as bad is the fact that she snores like a bear. Every time she breathes the windows rattle and the dishes in the kitchen crack and break. You'd have to be crazy to want to live with a woman like that. Not only will her breath make your skin peel, but her snoring is enough to wake up the dead.

Prince #3: Boy, that's unbelievable!

Prince #1: If you think that's bad, you should see what all the animals in the forest are doing. They're packing up and leaving in droves. Not only is she stinking up the air, but she's making the whole neighborhood shake with her snoring. It's getting to the point that nobody wants to be within five miles of the small cottage at the edge of the enchanted forest.

Prince #2: Well, how are we going to wake her up? Doesn't somebody have to kiss her, marry her, and live happily ever after in order for this story to end the right way?

Prince #1: Hey, maybe you pal … but not me! If you want to go ahead and kiss old "Hog's Breath," then help yourself. As for me, I'm going over to the next forest and see if I can get a date with Snow White; that is, if she's not going out with Grumpy, or Sneezy, or Dopey, or someone.

Narrator: And so it was that nobody wanted to kiss Sleeping Beauty. It wasn't until many years later, when mouthwash was invented, that a traveling salesman finally had the nerve to pour some mouthwash into Sleeping Beauty's mouth. He kissed her and she finally woke up. But, of course, she couldn't marry him because he was sort of stupid and ugly. So she spent the rest of her life living in the forest with a few squirrels and talking to lizards.

From *Frantic Frogs and Other Frankly Fractured Folktales for Readers Theatre* by Anthony D. Fredericks (Englewood, CO: Teacher Ideas Press, 1993), pp. 39–40. Used by permission of the author.

▶ Learn and Share

This form provides students with an opportunity to reflect on what they have read. It also offers students a chance to share their "learnings" with others—classmates, friends, or family members. It has particular appropriateness as an After Reading device because it can be completed as an individual activity or can be used as a group summary of a book read within a guided reading group. Duplicate this form and have it available when students finish the reading of content-specific materials. Plan sufficient time afterward to discuss the implications of what students read.

See page 183 for a sample form.

An Inside Look The bright lights of Las Vegas, Nevada, simmer on the horizon, but in Taro Yoshida's classroom there is a quiet atmosphere of intense learning and reflective introspection. Taro has been teaching for two years—her first year was in fifth grade and her second is in third grade. Born and raised just outside of Chicago, she moved to the West soon after her graduation from the University of Illinois. The large number of teaching jobs available, the warm climate, and the opportunity to see a new part of the country had attracted her.

Taro's classroom is one that celebrates reading as a natural and normal part of everyone's life. She infuses great books into each and every lesson—from art to science to social studies. Students enjoy Taro's lessons simply because they have an opportunity to listen to her read from a wide variety of literature and because Tao can relate that literature to their own lives.

One of the techniques Taro uses at the end of each week is the Learn and Share form. After a guided reading group has completed a specific book, Taro invites them to work together to complete individual copies of the Learn and Share form. Her objective is not to have everyone in a group arrive at the same responses, but rather to have them engage in some reflective thinking about the stories they have read. Students understand that this is not a formal assessment process, but rather a way for Ms. Yoshida to help them think deeply about what they read and how they can share that information with others. The result is a "community of learners" that celebrates the richness of good literature and honors the learning process. 📖

▶ Group Data Sheet

Whenever students work together in guided reading groups, it may be appropriate for a designated member of each group to complete a survey form similar to the Group Data Sheet on page 184. This form allows students to share and discuss their respective background knowledge, how they used that knowledge in "tackling" the subject matter of a book, what they discovered while reading the story, and some projections for the future. A form such as this places an emphasis on the Before, During, and After stages of the reading process and encourages students to comprehend their connections and relationships.

See page 276 for a sample lesson plan using this strategy.

▶ Student Self-Report Form

An effective guided reading group is one that involves youngsters throughout every aspect of the reading process, including assessment. When students participate in evaluating their own progress, they begin to develop an internal sense of responsibility, which helps them assume some degree of control over their own learning. A reading program that promotes student self-assessment is one in which teachers and students can work together to promote and evaluate activities and processes on an individual basis.

The Student Self-Report Form on page 185 can be duplicated and distributed to individual members of a guided reading group at the end of a week or upon completion of a book or story. After students have completed this form, provide sufficient opportunities for them, both individually and collectively, to discuss their responses to the items on the form. These discussions can help students appreciate the interactive role they can have with books and authors. In addition, students will begin to assume a level of responsibility that puts them "in control" of the reading process.

▶ Story Map

This "organizer" helps students determine the essential elements of a well-crafted story. Not only can students focus on important details (such as setting, characters, and problem), but more importantly, they begin to see how these "parts" of a story are woven together into a coherent whole. Equally significant is the fact that most well-written stories present some sort of problem for the main character or characters to solve. Students can begin to understand this often-used writing techniques by analyzing the elements of a story.

Provide individual copies of this sheet to the members of a guided reading group (an alternative plan would be to offer one sheet to the entire group; one student is the designated scribe while all group members contribute ideas). Encourage students to complete the form either while reading the story or (more appropriately) upon the completion of the story. Be sure to provide sufficient opportunities for students to share and discuss their respective interpretations of a story. It is not essential that students all arrive at the same conclusions, but rather that they have adequate opportunities to talk about their perceptions and conclusions.

A blank Story Map appears on page 186.

▶ Character Analysis

The Character Analysis form provides students with an opportunity to focus on the specific features, traits, or personality dynamics of individual characters within a story. This form may be used in one of two ways.

I. Provide each student in a guided reading group with a copy of the form on page 187. Invite each student to focus on the main character and to complete the form while reading the story and at the end of the story. Offer opportunities for students to discuss any differences of opinion in terms of individual perceptions of the same character.

2. Provide each student with a copy of the form and "assign" each person a different character from a book or story. Each student then completes her or his form and then discusses the "assigned" character with the other members of the guided reading group. Encourage students to discuss the elements or events that make some characters major and some character minor.

An Inside Look April Colucci has taught almost every elementary grade in her school in Princeton, New Jersey. To say that April is a dynamic teacher would be to state the obvious. Her classroom is filled with an array of learning materials, displays, and exhibits that would make most libraries or museums proud. She fills her rooms and the lives of her students with a wealth of scholastic endeavors that leaves her colleagues envious and her principal constantly amazed.

Her reading program is one that has developed from years of experimentation and attendance at lots of reading conferences and seminars. She has tried many techniques, incorporating some and rejecting others. Over the years she has developed what she refers to as "a comfortable system of borrowed ideas." One of those ideas is the Character Analysis form.

April uses this form throughout her guided reading program to assist her students in understanding the features and facts of selected story characters. April has discovered that the completion of this form enhances the collective work of a group in addition to providing selected individuals with a framework for analyzing significant characters. As described above, group members can each work on an individual character or a variety of characters. Completed forms can be added to student portfolios or used for individual student-teacher conferences.

▶ What If

Many of the questions we typically ask our students are of the literal or factual variety. There is an enormous body of research that suggests that students (at any grade) need to be exposed to a larger proportion of higher-level questions, divergent questions, and creative thinking questions. By doing so, we are ensuring that our students will be able to approach any reading task with a creative spirit, thus ensuring a dynamic interpretation of text.

One of the most effective strategies for promoting an active engagement with text is called 'What iffing." In this strategy, you take some of the questions that you would normally ask students at the conclusion of a guided reading passage and tag the two words "What if" to the front of each question. For example, instead of asking "Where did Brian (in *Hatchet*) live for 54 days?", an appropriate "What if" question would be "What if Brian had crashed in the desert?"

It is important to note that there are no right or wrong answers with "What iffing." Rather, students are given opportunities to "play" with language and the possibilities that might exist within a story or beyond that story. Students' divergent thinking is stimulated and enhanced in a wide variety of reading materials.

You will notice that "What if" questions encourage and stimulate the generation of multiple queries and multiple responses. Its advantage lies in the fact that all students are encouraged to participate and all responses can be entertained and discussed.

See page 211 for a sample lesson plan using this strategy.

An Inside Look   A group of teachers generated the following list of "What if" questions for the story "The Three Little Pigs." Here is a partial list of their queries:

What if the story was "The Three Little Wolves"?

What if all three houses had been made of brick?

What if the wolf had emphysema?

What if the story took place in the city?

What if the wolf kept kosher?

What if there was an army of pigs?

What if the story was told from the wolf's point of view? (Of course, this will lead to a discussion of *The True Story of the Three Little Pigs* by Jon Scieszka [New York: Viking, 1989].)

References

Fredericks, A. D. (1993). *Frantic frogs and other frankly fractured folktales for readers theatre.* Englewood, CO: Teacher Ideas Press.

Fowler, G. L. (1982). Developing comprehension skills in primary grades through the use of story frames. *The Reading Teacher,* 36(2), 176–179.

Gill, J. T., and Bear, D. (1988). No book, whole book, and chapter DRTA. *Journal of Reading,* 31, 444–449.

McGinley, W. J., and Denner, P. R. (1987). Story impressions: A pre-reading/writing activity. *Journal of Reading,* 31, 248–253.

Moore, D. W., and Moore, S. A. (1986). Possible sentences. *In Reading in the Content Areas: Improving Classroom Instruction,* 2nd ed., edited by E. K. Dishner, T. W. Bean, J. E. Readance, and D. W. Moore (pp. 174–179). Dubuque, IA: Kendall/Hunt.

Ogle, D. (1986). K-W-L: A teaching model that develops active reading of expository text. *The Reading Teacher,* 39, 564–570.

Stauffer, R. (1969). *Directing reading maturity as a cognitive process.* New York: Harper & Row.

Vacca, R., and Vacca, J. (1989). *Content area reading.* New York: HarperCollins.

Waldo, B. (1991). Story pyramid. In *Responses to Literature,* edited by J. M. Macon, D. Bewell, and M. Vogt (pp. 23–24). Newark, DE: International Reading Association.

Name _____ **Date** _____

Character Continuum

Book Title: _____

Character: _____

Friendly . . . . Unfriendly

Happy . . . . Sad

Popular . . . . Unpopular

Wise . . . . Foolish

Outgoing . . . . Shy

Unselfish . . . . Selfish

Sociable . . . . Unsociable

Ambitious . . . . Lazy

Neat . . . . Messy

Honest . . . . Dishonest

Brave . . . . Cowardly

Kind . . . . Cruel

Name   **Date**

Setting Continuum

Book Title: _____

Setting: _____

Hot .... Cold

Urban .... Rural

Friendly .... Hostile

Flat .... Hilly

Near Ocean .... Far from Ocean

Colorful .... Plain

New .... Old

Name _____ **Date** _____

Facts/Attitude Continuum

Book Title: _____

Topic: _____

Worldwide . . . . Limited

Alive . . . . Dead

Useful . . . . Harmful

Strong . . . . Weak

Neat . . . . Yucky

Eat Meat . . . . Eat Plants

Important . . . . Worthless

Live Birth . . . . Eggs

Not Poisonous . . . . Poisonous

Fun . . . . Boring

Underwater . . . . Above Water

Name _____

Date _____

Plot Graph

Book Title: _____

Author: _____

Character: _____

Personality Characteristic: _____

10

9

8

7

6

5

4

3

2

1

_____ _____ _____ _____

Summary: _____

_____

_____

_____

Name _____   **Date** _____

Book _____

Story Pyramid

Line 1:   Name of the main character
Line 2:   Two words describing the main character
Line 3:   Three words describing the setting
Line 4:   Four words stating the problem
Line 5:   Five words describing the main event
Line 6:   Six words describing a second main event
Line 7:   Seven words describing a third main event
Line 8:   Eight words stating the solution to the problem

1. _____

2. _____ _____

3. _____ _____ _____

4. _____ _____ _____ _____

5. _____ _____ _____ _____ _____

6. _____ _____ _____ _____ _____ _____

7. _____ _____ _____ _____ _____ _____ _____

8. _____ _____ _____ _____ _____ _____ _____ _____

Name _____   **Date** _____

Literature Log I

Book Title: _____

Author: _____

My favorite part was _____

_____

My least favorite part was _____

_____

The central problem was _____

_____

_____

_____

Some important words were _____

_____

Words I need to learn are _____

_____

My favorite character was _____

My least favorite character was _____

I didn't understand _____

I will never forget _____

I would recommend this book to _____ because _____

_____

_____

Name _____ **Date** _____

Literature Log II

Book Title: _____

Author: _____

Before Reading

I want to read this book because _____

_____

Here's what I know about this topic: _____

_____

These are some questions I would like to ask before I read: _____

_____

_____

I think the book is about _____

_____

During Reading

Here's what am I learning as I read this book: _____

_____

This is what I do when I didn't understand something in the book: ___

_____

I want to finish this book because _____

_____

_____

This is how I find answers to some of my questions: _____

The main character(s) is/are similar to some other(s) I have read

about: _____

This is why: _____

_____

After Reading

I think the author wrote this book because _____

_____

I am satisfied with this story because _____

_____

_____

I can write a brief summary of the story. _____

_____

_____

_____

_____

I would want to read this story at another time (yes/no). _____

There are questions I still need answers to: _____

_____

I will find that information here: _____

_____

The author could have made this a better book by _____

_____

_____

Name _____ **Date** _____

Book _____

Plot Frame

In this story the problem starts when _____

_____

_____

_____.

After that _____

_____

_____

_____.

Next, _____

_____

_____

_____.

Then, _____

_____

_____

_____.

The problem is finally solved when _____

_____

_____

_____.

Name _____ **Date** _____

Book _____

Information Frame

This story was written to teach us about _____
_____
_____
_____.

_____

One important fact I learned was _____
_____
_____.

Another fact I learned was _____
_____
_____.

A third important fact I learned was _____
_____
_____.

If I were to remember one important thing from this story, it would be _____
_____
_____

because _____
_____
_____.

Character Analysis Frame

_____ is an important character in this story.

_____ is important because _____

_____

_____.

Once, he/she _____

_____

_____

_____.

Another time, _____

_____

_____

_____.

    I think that _____ is _____

_____

because _____

_____.

He/she is also _____

_____

because _____

_____.

© 2001 Rigby

Name _____ **Date** _____

Book _____

Learn and Share

Three things I learned:

_____

_____

_____

_____

_____

_____

Two things I'd like to share with someone else:

_____

_____

_____

_____

_____

One thing I'd like to learn more about:

_____

_____

_____

_____

Name _____ **Date** _____

Group Data Sheet

Group members: _____

_____

Title of book read: _____

What we knew: _____

_____

_____

What we did: _____

_____

_____

What we discovered: _____

_____

_____

_____

What we still need to learn: _____

_____

_____

_____

The most interesting thing we learned: _____

_____

_____

Signed: _____

(Group Recorder)

Name _____   Date _____

Student Self-Report Form

Directions: Please complete this report about your reading activities this week. Your comments will form the basis for a discussion with me later:

Book: _____

_____

1. These are some of the things I learned this week: _____

_____

_____

2. These are some of the things that gave me trouble this week: _____

_____

_____

3. I believe I have improved this week. Here's why: _____

_____

_____

4. Here are some things I'd like to learn more about: _____

_____

_____

5. Here is how I would rate my performance this week: _____

_____

_____

6. This is what I'd like to do next week: _____

_____

_____

Name **Date**

Story Map

Title: _____

Setting:

Characters: _____

_____

Problem:

Event 1: _____

Event 2: _____

Event 3: _____

Event 4: _____

Solution:

Theme: _____

Name _____ **Date** _____

Character Analysis

Book Title: _____

Author: _____

In this story _____
(character's name)

is a _____ person.
(trait)

Several things happen to show that this is true. First, _____

_____

_____ .

Next, _____

_____

_____

Another time, _____

_____

_____ would probably have acted differently if

_____

_____

_____

or if _____

_____

_____ .

Literature Extensions

THIS SECTION OF THE BOOK is designed to provide you with a variety of extensions that offer students opportunities to become actively involved in the dynamics of individual books—empathizing with the characters, visualizing the settings, comprehending the plots and themes, and creatively experiencing the intentions of the author. It is critical to remember that the effective reading program is based on the opportunities children have to make an "investment of self." When students are provided with an arena that allows them to make choices and carry out those choices, then reading will become more personal and enjoyable. When we give students the chance to engage in a process of self-selection, we are telling them that they can become active decision-makers and "processors" of their own literacy growth.

Following are varied literature extensions that can be part of any guided reading program. They will be most effective when you give students opportunities to select those that meet their individual needs and interests. In short, they should not be *assigned*, but rather should be *offered*. In so doing, you will be helping students develop a measure of independence and autonomy within a guided reading lesson and eventually within all areas of your classroom curriculum.

Please feel free to alter or modify any of these suggestions in keeping with the dynamics of your own classroom and the individual strengths of students within a designated guided reading group. Allow students opportunities to alter or elaborate any activity according to their designs or creative responses. These suggestions are written to students instead of to the teacher. You may wish to collect them in a notebook or post them on a wall of the classroom for students to review periodically.

General Extension Activities

Use the following activities to extend the learning from any book or reading selection.

- Make up a colorful poster that "advertises" a collection of books by a designated author.
- Design and produce a puppet show based on a book. You may wish to videotape the show for others to enjoy.
- With other students create a simple play based on characters and/or scenes in the book.
- Create a new dust cover for a book. What events, characters, or settings would you include?
- Develop several magazine-type advertisements for a book. These advertisements can then be collected into a portfolio that can be distributed or sent around the school or district.
- Select a "reading buddy" and set aside a certain time during the day when the two of you can read to each other.
- Tape-record a portion of the book so other students can enjoy it.
- Illustrate the most exciting, the scariest, the saddest, or the happiest part of the book.
- Make a time chart of the six most important events in the book.
- Draw an imaginary setting for the book. What types of illustrations would you include in the book that are not there now?
- Make a crossword puzzle using the names, places, and events from the book.
- Write a series of questions that can be attached to the book for others to answer.
- Make a collage of important events in the book. Cut out pictures from old magazines and paste them on a sheet of construction paper.
- Work with some friends in writing a song for the book. Take one of your favorite songs and rewrite it using words from the book.
- Hold an "election" with members of your group for the favorite book of the month.
- Invent a comic strip using the characters and events in the book.
- Write a letter of appreciation to the author of the book telling him or her why you enjoyed it.

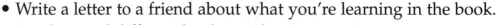

- Write a letter to a friend about what you're learning in the book.
- Read several different books on the same topic.
- Read several books by the same author.
- Make up a newspaper about the book.
- Create a fictional journal about a figure in the book.
- Write an original adaptation of an event.
- Set up a "Reading Corner" filled with periodicals, books, and other printed materials concerning the subject of the book.
- Record part of a book on cassette tape.
- Collect recipes the book characters might enjoy, and write a cookbook.
- Design a wordless picture book edition of the story.
- "Publish" an original adaptation of the book.
- Share the book with a classmate or partner.
- Design and write a newspaper article on an important event.
- Locate and read a relevant magazine article about something that happens in the book.
- Write an original play about an event in the book.
- Write a poem about something in the book.
- Write a letter to a character or historical figure.
- Write a sequel or prequel to an incident or event.
- Adapt an event into a news report or TV program.
- Create multiple endings for the book.
- Write a description of the book in 25 words or less, in 50 words or less, and in 75 words or less.
- Create interview questions for a guest speaker.
- Rewrite a portion of the book with students as major figures.
- Create a glossary or dictionary of important words in the book.
- Create a rebus story for younger students.
- Write riddles about events or circumstances in the book.
- Design a "Question Box" containing questions and answers based on the book.
- Print important phrases or quotations from the book on construction paper and post them throughout the room.
- Create a calendar of important events that took place in the story.
- Pretend you're a character in the book and write a letter to someone in your class.

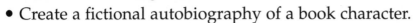

- Create a fictional autobiography of a book character.
- Write a travel guide for someone who wishes to journey to the setting of the book.
- Create a want ad for something in the book.
- Write a horoscope for a book character.
- Write a travel itinerary for visiting selected places in the book.
- Create a scrapbook about important places, people, and events in the book.
- Write a ten-question quiz for the book.
- Create a word bank of words from different parts of the book.
- Write a picture book (or wordless picture book) about a significant event from the book.
- Play a game of "20 Questions" about information in the book.
- Conduct a debate or panel discussion on an issue in the book.
- Interview outside "experts" in the local community about some information mentioned in the book.
- Create a new title for the book.
- Make up a list of information you'd still like to learn after reading the book.
- Make a story map of the book.
- Design a trivia game on book facts.
- Create a scale model of a particular location in the book.
- Create a time line of book events.
- Calculate the amount of time between various events.
- Create bar graph representations of sizes of characters.
- Measure distances on a map or globe.
- Design an imaginary blueprint of a building or house mentioned in the book.
- Calculate distances between places.
- Create word problems using distances between settings, sites, or other geographical areas mentioned in the book.
- Create a scale model of a place.
- Ask group members to rank-order their favorite characters in the book.
- Create a budget to travel to a place in the book.
- Create flash cards using illustrations from the book.

- Design a pictograph of book events.
- Create a graph or chart to record book data.
- Calculate the heights or weights of characters.
- Use a calendar to keep track of important dates in the book.
- Create a recipe a book character would enjoy.
- Create a family tree about a book character.
- Identify foods associated with different characters.
- Create an environmental guide to the setting in the book.
- Make a climate map of an area mentioned in the book.

- Trace the lives of certain characters.
- Create a display of different forms of transportation mentioned in the book.
- List important discoveries noted in the book.
- Build a scale model of a book character using clay or papier-mâché.
- Create a montage of different shelters/homes from the book.
- Create a replica of a historical site.
- Create an animal or plant scrapbook about species mentioned in the book.
- Create a display of different landforms in the book.
- Identify ecological concerns in the book's setting.
- Create a chart of weather patterns in different regions mentioned in the book.
- Write a logbook on the climate of an area.
- Construct a "self-history" scrapbook.
- Turn part of the book into a series of cartoons.
- Create a political cartoon about a significant event.
- Illustrate portions of the book.
- Make an advertisement about the book or story.
- Draw illustrations of each character in a book.
- Create a fashion magazine using book characters.
- Put together time capsules for different time periods from the book.

- Establish a "museum" of book artifacts in one corner of the classroom.
- Create a pop-up book about one important event.
- Make masks of different characters.
- Create an original slide show.
- Make a papier-mâché head of a major character.
- Design a new book cover.
- Make a "flip book" about selected events.
- Create a collage from old magazines.
- Design an original flannel board.
- Create a commercial to get others to read the book.
- Paint a large wall poster selling the book.
- Design and create a diorama of a significant scene.
- Create a three-dimensional display of artifacts associated with a story.
- Take photographs of similar scenes from the local community and arrange them into an attractive display.
- Make "movie rolls" using shoeboxes, adding machine tape, and pencils (as the "rollers").
- Assemble a collage of pictures.
- Plan a bulletin board of pictures cut out of old magazines.
- Design clay models of important characters.
- Locate paintings that relate to scenes mentioned in the book.
- Design a transparency about an important event and show it to the class.
- Create a salt map of a specific location.
- Develop an exercise program for a book figure.
- Create a "Question and Answer Relay" using specific book facts.
- Create a radio show about the book.
- Act out events in a story and videotape them.
- Design costumes for characters in a story.
- Pantomime selected events in a story.
- Sing folk songs associated with the book.
- Role-play a confrontation between two book characters.
- Present examples of music associated with various characters or settings.
- Take a popular song and rewrite the lyrics using words or phrases from a story.

- Role-play selected characters from a book.
- Design a filmstrip for a book (there are special filmstrip kits that you can obtain from educational bookstores).
- Give dramatic readings of a book.
- Select and include appropriate musical selections for an oral reading of the book.
- Create cassette recordings of related stories.
- Dramatize a section of the book for another class.
- Make up a scrapbook of "famous quotations" from the book.
- Write your reaction to the book on an index card and file it in a recipe box. Encourage others to do the same.
- Set up a panel discussion among several people who have read the same book.
- Make up several newspaper headlines about book events.
- List the qualities you like in a friend. Which book character comes closest to those qualities?
- Create a job "want ad" for one of the characters in the book.
- Create a "Wanted" poster for one or more book characters.
- Cut silhouettes of book characters from construction paper and retell the story to the members of your group.
- Explain which book character you would like to have as a next-door neighbor.
- Write to a pen pal in another classroom explaining what you like most and least about the book.
- Set up a TV news team to report on book events as they happen.
- Take on the role of a book character and write an autobiography.
- Write a movie script for a book.
- Write a readers theatre adaptation of the book.

Sample Extensions for Specific Books

Following are summaries of several popular children's books for Grades 3–6, each of which has a set of accompanying literature extensions. These extensions are possible additions to your own guided reading program and examples of the wide variety of "hands-on, minds-on" activities that can be used with students.

Summary: Like her grandfather, Alice Rumphius longs to travel around the world and live by the sea. Her grandfather advises her that she must also do one other thing; that is, to make the world more beautiful. Told from the perspective of Miss Rumphius's great-niece, it is a delightfully woven tale of one woman's determination to accomplish the goals she has set for herself during her lifetime.

Miss Rumphius

by Barbara Cooney
New York: Viking/Penguin, 1982
Level: 3B

1. Invite a student to create an original book on the history of sailing ships. She or he may wish to do some library research or create a model (store-bought or original) to use as a three-dimensional illustration.

2. Encourage a student to make a collage or poster of one of the countries hinted at in the book. This may include, but not be limited to, Switzerland, Kenya, Morocco, Tahiti, Australia, or any other countries that could have kangaroos, mountains, deserts, tropical environment, or lions.

3. A student may wish to make a tape recording of the book and loan it to the school library. If possible, he or she could add some sound effects (lions roaring, waves on a shore, winter winds) to the recording.

4. Invite a student to keep an ongoing daily journal of some of Miss Rumphius's journeys into distant lands.

5. Using a map of the world, a student can place push pins into all of the possible places Miss Rumphius could have visited during her travels.

6. Invite a student to investigate the various ways seeds are dispersed. Ask the student to determine if wind, water, or animal dispersal is the most efficient. (If possible, obtain "Seeds and How They Travel," a 16-minute filmstrip with cassette from The National Geographic Society [No. 04655].) Invite a botanist or college professor from a local college to explain the various ways seeds are dispersed.

7. Invite a student to investigate some of the major deserts of the world. What makes some of the deserts unique? How are deserts in the United States different from or similar to deserts in other parts of the world?

8. A student may wish to make a bulletin board display on how different types of mountains are created.

9. Bring in several different types of flower seeds, including lupines. Ask a student to grow the seeds (either outside or indoors using a "grow lamp"). Direct her or him to chart the different germination rates of the seeds as well as differences in the shape, color, and size of the resultant flowers. What makes lupines different from other types of flowers?

10. Encourage a student to create a make-believe dialogue between their grandparents and Miss Rumphius. What kinds of things would they talk about? What differences would there be in their childhood experiences?

11. Encourage a student to write a prequel or sequel to the story. What other events could have taken place after the story or before the story began?

12. Ask a student to check the yellow pages of the local phone book and compile a list of all the services related to elderly people (nursing homes, special equipment, social groups, etc.)

13. Invite a student to put together a scrapbook of different types of seashells. If the student has been to the ocean or lived by the sea, she or he may be able to provide some shells for others to enjoy.

14. Invite a student to create salt maps of her or his favorite place in the book. Use the following recipe:

> 4 cups flour
> 1 cup salt
> 1 $\frac{1}{2}$ cups warm water

Knead all the ingredients about 10 minutes. The mixture should be stiff but pliable. Spread out the mixture on a cookie sheet or piece of aluminum foil, forming it into various landform and ocean areas. Cook at 325° for about one hour or more depending on size. Brush with egg yolk mixed with one tablespoon of water and bake until very dry. Seal with two or three coats of polyurethane. Paint various areas with tempera paints and label.

15. Encourage a student to pretend that she or he is visiting one of the countries mentioned in the book. Ask the student to create a make-believe post-card to send back to her or his family at home. Post these cards on the bulletin board.

16. Invite a student to pretend that she or he is a news reporter for the local TV station. Ask the student to make up a series of questions to ask Miss Rumphius. Another student may wish to take on the role of Miss Rumphius to answer the questions.

17. Ask a student to interview her or his parents, grandparents, or relatives on family stories, folk tales, or legends that they learned as children. If some of these adults have immigrated from other countries, you may wish to invite them to visit your classroom to share some stories and legends from their country of origin.

18. Invite a student to write to the consulate or foreign embassy of some of the countries suggested in the book. The student can ask for travel details and other pertinent information that would be useful in planning a trip to those countries. The student can also prepare a travel plan for selected countries (length of stay, required documents/inoculations, necessary clothing, and so on).

19. Ask a student to create a sailing ship mobile. Using a coat hanger, the student can tie pieces of yarn to the hanger and pictures of different types of sailing ships to the yarn. The student may wish to create her or his own drawings of ships that can also be part of the mobiles.

20. A student may wish to create a shoebox diorama of a favorite scene from the story. Using construction paper, glue, toothpicks, cotton balls, clay, and other similar art materials, the student can create a wide variety of dioramas.

21. Ask a student to collect several types of seed catalogs. What differences and similarities exist between the various catalogs? Are prices for similar seeds comparable?

22. Students may wish to visit a local nursing home to talk with the residents about some of the adventures they had as children. Before the visit, talk to students about some of the questions they should ask the residents.

23. Provide the student with small balloons and ask her or him to blow up the balloons. The student should mix equal parts of liquid starch and water until the starch is dissolved. Then she or he can soak newspaper strips in the mixture and layer them over the balloons. When dry, the student can use tempera paints to outline areas of the globe and identify countries Miss Rumphius may have visited.

24. Invite a student to create an imaginary route for Miss Rumphius's travels. Have her or him plot this route on a map and calculate the distances between selected sites.

25. Encourage a student to create a poster or advertisement for visiting a particular place mentioned in the story. What facts, figures, data, or illustrations would need to be included in the "advertisement" in order to stimulate others to visit a particular destination?

26. Introduce a student to songs about the sea or old sailing songs. Check with your school's music teacher or the local public library for recordings of appropriate tunes.

27. Invite a student to create an exercise book for older adults. Which activities could be included? Which should be eliminated? The student may wish to check with a physical therapist or the physical education teacher.

28. Encourage a student to create costumes illustrating those worn by people mentioned in the story. What differences does she or he note in the costumes appropriate for warm countries as opposed to those costumes appropriate for colder climates?

29. Invite a student to create imaginary driver's licenses for some of the forms of transportation mentioned in the story. For example, what would a license to drive a camel look like? What about a license for a sailing ship?

30. Ask a student to collect several copies of travel magazines and prepare a collage of pictures clipped from those magazines. Each collage could focus on one of the countries Miss Rumphius visited during her journeys or could depict all possible countries.

31. Ask a student to look in the telephone directory and create a list of all the services Miss Rumphius may have needed prior to her journeys. For example, a travel agent, a clothing store, a doctor, and a bookstore are possibilities. The student may wish to create her or his own special Yellow Pages specifically for Miss Rumphius.

Mufaro's Beautiful Daughters

by John Steptoe
New York: Lothrop, Lee and Shepard, 1987
Level: 4D

Summary: Mufaro lived in a small village in Africa with his two beautiful daughters, Nyasha and Manyara. Nyasha was kind and considerate, while Manyara was selfish and spoiled. When the king announces he is looking for the most beautiful daughter in the land to be his wife, Manyara is determined to reach the city before her sister. The ending is a lesson for us all as kindness prevails over greed.

1. Read the introductory page of the story to the students, explaining the meanings of the characters' names in the story. The student can then dramatize her or his favorite parts of the story.

2. Invite several students to sit down in a circle and sing "Kumbaya," a traditional African folk song (see *The Book of Kidsongs* by Nancy and John Cassidy [Palo Alto, CA: Klutz Press, 1986]).

3. Encourage a student to create puppets of the story characters by decorating old socks with markers, colored paper, bits of yarn, or other scraps. Invite the student to create a mini-play about a specific scene on the book.

4. Provide a student with old white bed sheets and fabric scraps. Using the book as a guide, invite the student to create a costume like the ones worn by the characters in the story. The student can then dramatize her or his favorite parts of the story.

5. Read the poem "African Dance" by Langston Hughes aloud to a group. Read it again and encourage students keep a steady beat with the rhythm of the poem by beating homemade drums, clapping hands, or using other rhythm instruments.

6. Have an African foods celebration. Bring in a variety of foods native to Africa: honey, dates, coffee, cloves (try clove gum), yams, sunflower seeds, peanuts, grapes, and olives. Group students and ask each group to write a paragraph describing their reactions to the foods.

7. Hang a large world map on one wall of the room. Encourage a student to plot a travel route to Africa by making a cardboard ship and marking her or his trip (on the map) with yarn. Attach the ship so that it can travel freely along the string from the United States to Africa. The student may wish to write a story describing her or his feelings as she or he begins the trip to Africa.

8. Working in pairs, invite students to construct models of one of the houses found in Africa: thatched roof huts, apartment houses, houses on stilts, adobe houses, or nomadic tents. Students will need to consult appropriate library books for ideas.

9. Invite a student to plant sunflower seeds in empty margarine tubs. Keep the lids on until the seeds have sprouted. Remove the lids and place the tubs in a sunny window. Ask the student to generate a list of all the products that are made from sunflowers. If possible, plant the seedlings on the school grounds. The student can tend the plants until they are ready to be harvested.

10. Read the book *Why Mosquitoes Buzz in People's Ears* by Verna Aardema (New York: Dial Press, 1975). Explain to students that this is an African folk tale just as *Mufaro's Beautiful Daughters* is an African folk tale. Ask students to compare the two stories and work with a partner to generate a list of similarities and differences between the two stories.

11. Invite a student to write a sequel to the story entitled "How Manyara Learned Kindness."

12. Ask a student to create a list of the various ways in which she or he shows respect to other people (including family members). What are some customs that everyone follows? What are some optional customs? Why is it important to demonstrate respect for other people?

13. Students may enjoy preparing *kanya*, a popular sweetmeat in many West African countries, using the following recipe:

Thoroughly mix ½ cup smooth peanut butter and ½ cup superfine sugar in a large bowl. Press any granules of sugar against the sides of the bowl with a wooden spoon until they are completely crushed and mixed with the peanut butter. Slowly add ⅔ cup of uncooked Cream of Rice® and continue stirring until the mixture is completely and thoroughly blended. Spread the mixture in a loaf pan and press down with both hands until it is evenly spread. Cover the pan with plastic wrap and refrigerate for two to three hours until firm. Cut into small bars with a knife and enjoy.

Summary: Leigh Botts writes to his favorite book author. His letters are filled with questions and advice as well as a lot of revealing information about Leigh's life, his thoughts, and his feelings about his mother and father. This is a touching tale, told strictly through the correspondence of one boy, that offers a realistic and humorous look at the struggles of growing up.

Dear Mr. Henshaw
by Beverly Cleary
New York: Morrow, 1983
Level: 5B

1. Invite a student to read other books by Beverly Cleary. Although there are many, here are a few to get her or him started: *Henry and Beezus* (New York: Morrow, 1952); *Mitch and Amy* (New York: Morrow, 1967); *Ramona the Pest* (New York: Morrow, 1968); and *Ramona Quimby, Age 8* (New York: Morrow, 1981).

2. Ask a student to create her or his own electronic gadgets much like Leigh did. Look for kits at your local electronics store. For students interested in constructing their own burglar alarm, Natural Science Industries produces the "Electro-Tech Kit" (available through science catalogs), which allows children to create a variety of electrical objects. A fascinating book for kids is *The X-Ray Picture Book of Everyday Things and How They Work* by Peter Turvey (New York: Watts, 1995).

3. Invite a student to contact local trucking firms and ask for the number of miles (or number of hours) their drivers are allowed to drive over a 24-hour period. With that data, invite the student to figure out all the cities that can be reached from her or his town if a driver were to stay within the designated parameters. What towns could Leigh's father drive to (from Pacific Grove, California) with the time and distance restrictions?

4. A student may wish to read about the life and writings of Beverly Cleary. Your school or local librarian will be able to supply several references. One particularly useful source is the author's own story, *A Girl from Yamhill* (New York: Morrow, 1988).

5. Encourage students to put together a large mural on the history of transportation in this country. Several pairs of students could work in gathering the necessary research for one aspect of transportation (land, air, sea travel). Information, pictures, brochures, photos and the like can all be posted on the mural, which can be displayed in the school library.

6. One or more students may be interested in watching the development and growth of butterflies. Nasco (901 Janesville Ave., Fort Atkinson, WI 53538 [800-558-9595]) produces the Butterfly Garden, which can be ordered through their catalog or can be found in many toy and hobby stores. Students will be able to observe and record the growth of butterflies from cocoons to adults.

7. Invite a student to put together a guidebook entitled "How to Become a Better Writer." Invite her or him to interview adults, teachers, businesspeople, reporters, and other children in the community on the tips and strategies that help people write. The student can assemble the information into a booklet to be distributed to other classes.

8. Invite a student to put together an oversized collage of trucks and the trucking industry. Using pictures from old magazines as well as information and brochures collected from local trucking firms, a student can assemble an informative collage for posting in the classroom or a wall of the school.

9. Invite a student to compute the number of miles from Leigh's home in Pacific Grove, California, to some of the other cities mentioned in the book (such as Bakersfield, California; Taft, California; Albuquerque, New Mexico; and Hermiston, Oregon). Later, invite the student to figure out the number of miles between each of those cities and her or his school. These figures can be posted on a large classroom map of the United States.

10. A student may be interested in obtaining travel and tourist information about California. She or he can write to Office of Tourism, Box 189, Sacramento, CA 95812-0189. When material arrives, the students should arrange it into an attractive display.

11. Invite a student to check the audio sections of her or his local library or college library for recordings or songs dealing with trucks or truck drivers (country/western songs might be a logical place to begin). Invite the student to put together a listing or series of recordings of trucking songs to share with classmates. What is distinctive about these songs?

12. Invite a student to prepare a letter to Beverly Cleary commenting on this book or any other(s) she has written. The student may wish to include questions about the writing of children's books or about writing in general. Send the letter in care of Ms. Cleary's publisher (William Morrow and Co., 105 Madison Ave., New York, NY 10016). Advise the student that since Ms. Cleary receives so much mail, they may not receive a personal reply, but there's certainly no harm in trying. (By the way, Beverly Cleary's birthday is April 12—one or more students may wish to send her a birthday card.)

13. A student may wish to learn about children's book authors and how they write their books. Invite a student to log on to the following author website to learn about the writing process: www.afredericks.com/author/index.html.

Sadako and the Thousand Paper Cranes

by Eleanor Coerr
New York: Putnam's, 1977
Level: 6B

Summary: Sadako was two years old when the atom bomb was dropped on Hiroshima. Although she was not injured during the bomb attack, she became ill with leukemia ten years later. A friend told Sadako that if she folded 1,000 paper cranes, they would bring her good luck and she would live a long life. Sadako died before she could fold all the cranes, but her classmates folded the remainder and they were buried with Sadako.

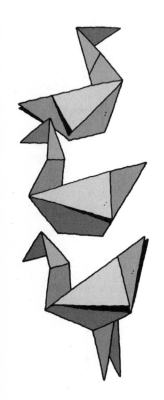

1. This book talks about several good luck signs. Invite s student to create an original good luck charm and write a paragraph to go with it. The paragraph can be written in the form of the daily horoscope column from the newspaper.

2. Encourage a student to read the book *The Faithful Elephants* by Yukion Tsuchiya (Boston: Houghton Mifflin, 1988). Invite the student to summarize the story from an animal's viewpoint.

3. A student may be interested in reading books about the human body. Here are a few to get started: *Blood and Guts: A Working Guide to Your Own Insides* by Linda Allison (Boston: Little, Brown, 1976); *Our Bodies* by Robert Brown (Milwaukee, WI: Gareth Stevens, 1990); *The Body Atlas* by Mark Crocker (New York: Oxford University Press, 1991); *Outside and Inside You* by Sandra Markle (New York: Bradbury Press, 1991); and *The Human Body and How It Works* by Angela Royston (New York: Random House, 1990).

4. The human skeleton continues to grow until sometime between the ages of 16 and 22. Invite a student to record the heights of her or his respective family members. This can be done once each month. Encourage the student to make predictions about each family member's height for the forthcoming month. Which persons in the family are continuing to grow? Who has stopped growing? The student may wish to create a special chart or graph of family members' heights over time. Friends and other relatives can be added to the chart.

5. Assign a student a specific human disease. Challenge the student to locate as much outside information as possible about the causes and cures for the selected illness. Invite the student to assemble her or his data in the form of brochures or leaflets that can be distributed throughout the school. Local health organizations also offer some preliminary data.

6. Work with a student to make a map of Japan using burlap. Cut a large piece of blue burlap to serve as the base and to represent the ocean. Cut another piece of burlap in a different color in the shape of the island of Japan. Invite the student to make a key and sew symbols on the map with yarn and simple stitches. Attach bodies of water, large cities, lines of latitude and longitude, and the island itself to the base, leaving an opening of 4 inches. Stuff a thin layer of polyester fiberfill into the picket between island and base (this will give the map a 3-D effect). Sew the opening shut.

7. A student may enjoy making this popular Japanese dish:

Black and White Salad
(makes enough for 4 people)

4 to 6 leftover boiled potatoes	pinch of dill
2 Tbsp. white vinegar	mace
juice from $1/2$ lemon	1 can cooked mussels
salt and pepper	1 can button mushrooms
parsley (large handful)	walnut halves

Slice potatoes. Mix the next four ingredients and marinate potatoes in the mixture. Add a pinch of dill and a little powdered mace. Drain the mussels and the mushrooms. Mix gently with potatoes. Garnish with a few walnut halves.

After the student has made the recipe, invite her or him to calculate the quantities of ingredients that would be necessary in order to make enough for 20 people, 65 people, everybody at your grade level, or any other large group of people.

8. Invite a student to work with the music teacher to put together a collection of traditional Japanese music to share with classmates. Invite the student to note some of the distinctive qualities or characteristics of traditional Japanese music and how it differs from traditional Western music.

9. Invite students to select a song or tune that would be appropriate to play while reading this story out loud (see number 1 above) to another group of students. Is there a song that would capture the tone or mood of the story without interfering with its theme?

10. Obtain photocopies of major newspapers from 1945 reporting the drop of the bomb and its effects. (A local college library or newspaper company could supply these.) Invite a student to use this information to write a radio announcement reporting the event. Encourage the student to record the announcements onto a tape recorder, if one is available.

11. Invite a student to write to several travel agencies to get information about a trip to Japan. The student can ask about different ways to get there, length of stay, whether meals are included in the price, if guided tours are included, prices, and so on. Encourage the student to make a chart comparing the information from the agencies.

12. Sadako was taken to a Red Cross hospital. A student may want to visit a local office of the American Red Cross. Invite her or him to ask for information about what the Red Cross does and how citizens can help.

– – – – – – – – –

The Literature Extensions provided in this section of the book are designed to open up learning possibilities for any literature-based guided reading lesson. Feel free to select, adapt, or modify these suggestions in keeping with the needs and abilities of individual students as well as members of a specific guided reading group. Also, be sure to provide students with multiple opportunities to select activities and learning opportunities that have meaning for them. In doing so, you will be providing them with a personal stake in their individual literacy development. Obviously, no single literature extension is appropriate for every student in a group; nor should all students within a group attempt to complete identical activities. There are many interpretations of literature, and students should be allowed to pursue and elaborate activities that will enhance their appreciation of a specific piece of literature.

Lesson Plans

THIS SECTION OF THE BOOK provides you with 28 lesson plans for selected pieces of children's literature, including books from a variety of genres, reading levels, and interest levels. You will discover both expository and narrative books as well as Caldecott and Newbery medalists, Reading Rainbow selections, Booklist and Horn Book recommendations, and teacher recommendations from around the country. Here you will find a wide range of titles and the various ways in which *any* piece of literature can be incorporated into the guided reading program.

Each of the following lesson plans uses the format presented earlier in this book. This format (see below) is organized into five separate categories that allow you to "slot" appropriate instructional activities into a dynamic and engaging framework for guided reading.

Setting the Stage	
Before Reading	
During Reading	
After Reading	
Literature Extensions	

The lesson plans that follow use a separate and individual reading strategy for each designated book. The selection of a particular strategy was arbitrary and was not based on any specific criteria (other than its appropriateness for expository or narrative literature). It is my hope that you will see how the various strategies in this book can be combined with a diversity of titles to assist students within and throughout their guided reading encounters. In short, the "assignment" of a designated strategy to a designated book is based more on a teacher's decision about what is best for her or his individual students than it is on any preconceived standards established by one or more outside "experts."

You will discover a wide range of instructional possibilities within this section of the book, and you will also discover the flexibility that can be part and parcel of a guided reading program. Use these lesson plans as guides rather than absolutes. Adapt, modify, and alter these lessons according to the needs of your students and the evolving nature of your classroom. Also, use these plans as blueprints for the design and delivery of your own lessons with your own literature.

Low Third Grade

Summary: It is the first day of school. A young boy wonders who his teacher will be. Imagine his surprise (and that of his classmates) when the teacher turns out to be a fearsome green creature with claws and a fiery breath. Horrible things happen to several children, yet the principal seems unconcerned. A surprise ending adds to the hilarity in this delightful and imaginative book, which is sure to be a classroom favorite.

The Teacher from the Black Lagoon

by Mike Thaler
New York: Scholastic, 1989
Level: 3A

Setting the Stage

Before distributing copies of the book to the members of a guided reading group, share the title with students. Invite students to make predictions about the story. What will it be about? Who will be in it? How will it turn out?

Before Reading

Engage students in a What-If activity (see page 169). Ask each student to imagine that they had a teacher from the Black Lagoon. What would she or he look like? What would the teacher do? How would students behave in a classroom that had a teacher from the Black Lagoon? You may wish to "stir the pot" a little by asking some of the following questions:

What if your teacher was from the Black Lagoon?

What if the school was filled with teachers from the Black Lagoon?

What if the principal was from the Black Lagoon?

What if the person sitting next to you was from the Black Lagoon?

What if the Black Lagoon was outside our classroom?

During Reading

Provide a copy of the book for each student. Ask students to read the book silently on their own.

After Reading

Encourage students to talk about the humor in this book. What does the author do to make this a funny book? How did the illustrations contribute to the humor in the book? Did anything happen that you didn't expect? You may want to follow the reading by asking students some of the same questions you did in the "Before Reading" stage. Invite students to share reasons for any changes in their responses.

Literature Extensions

Invite students to select one or more of the following:

1. Encourage students to create their own original stories about their "Teacher from the Black Lagoon." Later, students can create stories or develop a skit on "The Mother/Father from the Black Lagoon."

2. Have students create a guidebook on the qualities of a good teacher. What makes a teacher "outstanding"? What do teachers need to know about children? What do teachers need to know about the learning process? If possible, make arrangements with the teacher education program at a nearby college to donate the guidebooks to their library or share it with pre-service teachers in a methods course.

3. Invite students to prepare an advertisement or commercial promoting the book to friends or students in another class. What type of information should be included to "sell" the book to others? Should the advertisement/commercial be humorous or serious?

4. Encourage students to create their own sequel to the book. How might the story continue? What other school personnel live in "the Black Lagoon"? Introduced the other books in the series: *The Principal from the Black Lagoon, The Gym Teacher from the Black Lagoon, The Cafeteria Lady from the Black Lagoon*, and so on.

The True Story of the Three Little Pigs

by Jon Scieszka
New York: Penguin, 1989
Level: 3B

Summary: A riotous retelling of the classic tale about the big bad wolf and the three little pigs—except this time the wolf gets to tell his side of the story. The wolf acts as his own reporter just to make sure the facts are correct, and the result is an uproariously funny story that kids will want to read over and over again.

Setting the Stage

Invite students to share their memories of the "Three Little Pigs" story. Who are the major characters? What role does the wolf play? How does the story end?

Before Reading

Invite students to construct a Five Circles diagram (see page 136) and to fill in each of the circles with information or details from their collective memory of the Three Little Pigs story. Students may wish to complete the Five Circles in pairs or as a group. Inform students that they will be doing another Five Circles diagram after reading this book.

During Reading

Provide students with individual copies of the book and invite them to read it silently. Assist students with any difficult vocabulary or concepts during the reading process.

After Reading

Invite students to construct another Five Circles diagram using the characters, plot, theme, and details from *The True Story of the Three Little Pigs.* Afterward, encourage students to compare their original diagram with the diagram developed for the book. Plan time for students to discuss any similarities and/or differences. Encourage students to discuss what Jon Scieszka did to make this book so hilarious.

Literature Extensions

Invite students to select one or more of the following:

1. Have students select one or more familiar stories (such as "The Three Billy Goats Gruff," "Little Red Riding Hood," "Cinderella," or "Hansel and Gretel"). Encourage them to retell or rewrite a version of the selected story from the point of view of a different character. For example, "Cinderella" could be told from the point of view of one of the stepsisters. Plan time for students to share their retellings with other members of the class.

2. Ask students to select a favorite nursery rhyme or fairy tale and write it as a newspaper article. In other words, how would a newspaper reporter write a story about a little girl (in a red riding hood) traveling through the forest on her way to her grandmother's house?

3. Invite students to create an oversized collage of pig pictures and illustrations cut from several different magazines. How many different versions of pigs can they locate?

4. If possible, obtain a copy of the National Geographic video *Animals on the Farm* (catalog no. A51498; http://www.nationalgeographic.com or 1-800-368-2728). Discuss with students the importance of farms to the economy of the country and the contributions of farmers to our everyday lives.

5. Invite students to work with the school's music teacher to compile a collection of songs related to pigs and farm animals. Plan opportunities when students can share these songs in class

6. Invite students to create a wordless picture book using important events from the story. What challenges are there in creating a wordless version of this story? What will students need to consider in order to maintain the humor in the story?

High Third Grade

Summary: One day Alexander wakes up with gum in his hair. From then on, the whole day is filled with one misfortune after another. He wants to move to Australia, but he realizes terrible days happen everywhere, even in Australia. This long-standing favorite of teachers and students is a perfect complement to any guided reading program and lends itself to a wide range of extending activities.

Alexander and the Terrible, Horrible, No Good, Very Bad Day

by Judith Viorst
New York: Macmillan, 1972
Level: 3C

Setting the Stage

Provide each student with a copy of the book. Record the title of the book on the chalkboard and invite group members to ask questions about the title or the contents of the book. Record all questions.

Before Reading

Guide students through the Student Motivated Active Reading Technique (S.M.A.R.T.) (see page 98). Based on the questions written on the chalkboard, encourage the group to make one or more predictions about the plot of the book. Students also decide on the questions they feel to be most appropriate for exploration. Invite students to read the book independently.

During Reading

Ask students to examine all of the illustrations in the book and to pose additional questions during the reading process. Add these questions to those already on the board. Based on the list of questions recorded, ask students to generate additional predictions about the story line. Students continue to read, searching for answers to some of their previously posed queries. As they find answers, the students talk about them and attempt to arrive at agreeable responses.

After Reading

Upon completion of the book, students discuss all recorded questions and answers provided in the book. The group decides on appropriate answers. Questions that were not answered from the text are also shared. Encourage students to refer back to the book to answer any lingering questions.

Literature Extensions

Invite students to select one or more of the following:

1. Students write a brief essay about a recent horrible day. What happened? How did they feel? Ask each student to share the essay with other class members.

2. Encourage students to write an alternate version of the story entitled, "Alexander and the Wonderful, Terrific, Super, Fantastic Day." Students may wish to record the story on audio tape for others to enjoy.

3. Invite students to become advice columnists. Ask them to suggest some strategies or solutions for Alexander to consider in dealing with his terrible day.

4. Have students interview an adult about the worst day that individual ever had. Students may wish to interview a parent, baby-sitter, or neighbor. Encourage students to share the results of their interviews with the rest of the class.

5. Ask students to create an imaginary time line of all of the activities and events in this story. They can print selected events along a length of adding-machine tape. They can print a time of day over each event as well. Encourage students to defend their choice of times and the corresponding event(s). The strips of paper can be posted on a bulletin board.

6. Invite students to obtain some materials and resources on Australia from the library. Encourage them to put together a descriptive brochure on the climate, animals, lifestyles, geography, and other aspects of the country.

Summary: Grace loves stories, but she especially loves to act out stories. When there's an opportunity to play a part in the school play, Peter Pan, Grace wants to be the lead character. Everyone tells her she can't, but with the loving support of her mother and wise grandmother, Grace learns that she can be anything she wants to be, and the results are amazing. This book wonderfully celebrates the human spirit and is a "must have" for any classroom and any child.

Amazing Grace

by Mary Hoffman
New York: Dial Books for Young Readers, 1991
Level: 3C

Setting the Stage	Show students the four illustrations on the title page of the book. Invite students to make some predictions about Grace. What kind of person do you think Grace is? What kinds of things does she like to do? Is Grace similar to anyone you know?
Before Reading	Read the first page of the book aloud to the students. Invite students to discuss Grace. How does the first page of the book compare with some of their initial predictions about Grace (see above)? Do any of their predictions change as a result of hearing the first page of the book? Invite students to discuss the last sentence on the first page. What are some exciting parts that Grace could play?
During Reading	Ask students to read the book in its entirety. As students read, invite them to complete a Feelings Web (see page 135) to record some of the emotions Grace goes through during the story. What different emotions did she experience?
After Reading	Encourage students to review all of the emotions recorded on their respective Feelings Webs. Invite students to each share a time in their lives when they experienced one of the emotions that Grace experi-

enced. Did their reactions parallel those of Grace or were they different? Did anyone help them "get through" those emotions as Grace's grandmother helped her?

Literature Extensions

Invite students to select one or more of the following:

I. Have each child create a portrait of himself or herself in the role of a well-known character from a popular book. What characters do they choose? What traits make the character an appropriate choice? Plan time for students to post their characters and discuss their selections.

2. As a read-aloud book, share *Peter Pan* with the students. Invite them to discuss any similarities between *Peter Pan* and *Amazing Grace*. What personal qualities does each book emphasize?

3. Encourage students to write a sequel to *Amazing Grace* from the perspective of the original narrator or from that of Grace herself. They could also write the sequel from the perspective of Grace's class (one or more students) and their newfound perceptions of this remarkable girl.

Summary: In the land of Chewandswallow, the weather brings showers of food and drink for the people three times a day. One day the weather gets out of control, raining massive quantities of food, and forces the people of Chewandswallow to find a new land to call their home.

Cloudy with a Chance of Meatballs

by Judi Barrett
New York: Macmillan, 1978
Level: 3C

Setting the Stage	Invite students to briefly discuss how they would feel if they never had a choice of what to eat for breakfast, lunch, or dinner.
Before Reading	Create a transparency of the illustration on the cover of the book. Project the transparency of the two separate groups using the Picture Perfect strategy (see page 115). Invite members of each group to generate three to five questions about the illustration. Ask the groups to exchange their questions with each other. Invite each group to create a story that has answers to the other group's questions embedded in the story. Invite the groups to share their completed stories with each other.
During Reading	Invite students to read the entire book. Ask them to pay attention to the way in which the illustrator began with black-and-white illustrations, slowly added some color as the story progressed, and ended with black-and-white illustrations at the end.
After Reading	Invite each of the two groups to return to their original "Picture Perfect" stories and to edit them in light of the information they gathered from the book. What changes will they need to make in a second or third draft?

Literature Extensions

Invite students to select one or more of the following:

1. Ask students to gather newspaper and magazine articles about weather or bring in daily weather forecasts from local newspapers or TV news shows. Place articles in shoeboxes and share them in a "weather news" area.

2. If possible, invite selected students to take photographs of various cloud patterns. When the photos are developed, ask students to arrange them into an attractive display for the entire class. Students may wish to include descriptions of each cloud type and what it means in terms of impending weather.

3. If possible, take students on a field trip to the local supermarket. Invite them to locate the prices of all the foods mentioned in the story. Encourage them to figure out the cost of a single meal as illustrated in the book.

4. In the book there is a newspaper with current events. Have students make a "food newspaper" about food, cooking, meals, and other eating events that take place at home. How can dinner be turned into a sporting event? How can breakfast be turned into front-page news?

Summary: This is a touching story about a young boy and his father who are homeless and live in an airport. The book tells how they elude security people, obtain food, and learn to survive by their wits. A poignant story, it is filled with hope and determination for a better life. This is a wonderful read-aloud story for every classroom.

Fly Away Home

by Mike Thaler
New York: Clarion, 1991
Level: 3C

Setting the Stage	Provide copies of the book to each student. Invite students to "thumb" through the book and look at all the illustrations. What can they share about the people in the book? Where does this story take place? Are any of the people or the setting similar to people or an airport they've seen before?
Before Reading	Provide students with a Divergent Semantic Web (see page 95) with the word *Homelessness* written in the center. Ask each student to write words, phrases, or concepts related to *homelessness* on the spokes of the web. After students have done this individually, ask them to compile their ideas into a large web that focuses on homelessness. Note any misperceptions or biases students may have.
During Reading	Invite students to read the book silently. "Visit" each student and provide any assistance as needed. Help students with difficult vocabulary (such as *Security*, *terminal*, and *escalators*) as necessary.
After Reading	Invite students to return to their original semantic web. Using a different color of ink, ask students (individually at first, then as a group) to add words or terms from the book to the original web. Plan time for students to discuss any differences in their pre-reading knowledge about homelessness and their post-

reading knowledge about homelessness. How have their perceptions changed as a result of reading the book?

Literature Extensions

Invite students to select one or more of the following:

1. Have students write a letter to the editor of the local newspaper about the plight of homeless people in this country.

2. Encourage students to write a fictitious letter to the young boy in the story. What words of support can students share with the boy that would give him hope for a better future?

3. Ask students to write a sequel to the story. What happens to the boy and his father in one month? In one year? In five years? Be sure to plan time for students to share their stories.

4. Encourage students to create individual scrapbooks of all the places they have lived during their lives. Have students collect photos from old magazines and assemble them into various categories (houses, apartment buildings, trailer parks, etc.).

Summary: A young man enters the rain forest to cut down a kapok tree, but before he knows it the heat makes him tired and weak. The man sits down to rest and falls asleep. While he sleeps, the animals of the forest whisper in his ear not to cut down the kapok tree. Each animal has a different reason. Upon awakening, the man realizes the importance of the kapok tree.

The Great Kapok Tree

by Lynne Cherry
San Diego: Gulliver Books, 1990
Level: 3D

Setting the Stage	Share a map of the world with students. Point out the location of Brazil and the area encompassed by the Brazilian rain forest. Provide each student with an individual copy of the book.
Before Reading	Lead students through a mental imagery activity. Ask them to close their eyes and imagine that they are deep in a Brazilian rain forest. Ask them to imagine the various types of plants and the different types of animals they would see in the rain forest. Ask them to imagine the temperature and the humidity. Ask them to think about the sounds of the rain forest. Have them open their eyes and describe some of the "mind pictures" they created
During Reading	Read the first two pages of the book aloud to students. Afterward, have students read the rest of the book silently.
After Reading	Upon completion of their silent reading, pair students. Ask each pair to complete an Information Story Frame (see page 160). After each pair has completed their respective frame, plan time for the pairs to share and compare the information they recorded. What similarities and/or differences do the pairs note in the

frames? Plan time to discuss the one important thing each student learned from the story.

Literature Extensions

Invite students to select one or more of the following:

1. Have each student assume the role of one of the creatures in the story and write a thank-you note to the man for sparing the tree.

2. Ask students to rewrite the ending of the story and tell what would have happened if the man *had* cut down the tree.

3. Invite students to make a collage of all the animals in the book. They may wish to cut out photographs and illustrations from a collection of old magazines or environmental catalogs. The collages can be posted throughout the classroom or school.

4. The rain forest is filled with an enormous variety of birds. Students may wish to create a series of bird feeders and compare the birds in their part of the country with those that inhabit the rain forest.

5. Students may wish to grow some rainforest plants in the classroom. Invite them (with their parents) to visit a large supermarket, garden shop, or nursery and look for one or more of the following rainforest plants: African violet, begonia, bird's-nest fern, croton, dumb cane, philodendron, prayer plant, or zebra plant.

Summary: In the countryside of northern China, a woman lived with her three daughters. One day, because she had to leave the house to visit her daughters' granny, she warned her children not to open the door or let anyone in. Soon after her departure, a wolf visits the house in the disguise of the grandmother. With wit and wisdom, the three children are able to dispatch the wolf. This is a marvelously illustrated Chinese version of the classic tale "Little Red Riding Hood."

Lon Po Po: A Red Riding Hood Story from China

by Ed Young
New York: Philomel, 1989
Level: 3D

Setting the Stage

Ask students if they are familiar with the story of Little Red Riding Hood. Invite them to share their remembrances of that story. If students have not heard the story, take a few minutes to read a classic version of the story to them.

Before Reading

Provide each student with a copy of the book. Ask students to look through the book quickly, paying attention to the descriptive illustrations. What kinds of feelings do the illustrations evoke? How are the illustrations different from those in other books? Tell students that this book won the Caldecott Medal for the best illustrated children's book of 1989. Ask them to pay close attention to the illustrations as they read the book.

During Reading

Invite students to read the book independently from start to finish. Circulate and provide individual attention where necessary.

After Reading

After students have finished reading the book, invite them to participate in the Readers Theatre script that follows: *Little Red Riding Hood and the Big Bag Wolf Have a Friendly Conversation (Finally)*. (See also page 163.)

Literature Extensions

Invite students to select one or more of the following:

1. Students may be interested in listening to a self-advancing slide presentation (with audio) of the original version of "Little Red Riding Hood." They can do so by logging on to http://www.ipl.org/youth/StoryHour/goose/ridinghood.

2. Students may wish to work together to create a large wall mural recounting important scenes from the story. Obtain a large sheet of newsprint from a local hobby store or newspaper office. Using tempera paints, students can work together to illustrate the scenes.

3. Invite students to retell the story from the perspective of the wolf. What were some of the things the wolf observed or thought about? How would the wolf's version of the story be different from a version told by one of the three daughters or the version told by the narrator?

4. Invite students to assume the roles of newspaper reporters and to report on the events in *Lon Po Po* as though they were part of the local newspaper. What are some significant events, background information (real or imaginary), or photographs (illustrations) that could be included in a *Lon Po Po* newspaper?

5. Obtain a copy of *Yeh Shen: A Cinderella Story from China*, which is illustrated by Ed Young. How does Yeh Shen compare with the version of Cinderella with which your students are most familiar? Are there any comparisons between that book and *Lon Po Po*?

Little Red Riding Hood and the Big Bad Wolf Have a Friendly Conversation (Finally)

Staging: The narrator sits far behind the two characters. The characters can stand in front of the audience or sit on two tall stools.

Narrator
X

Little Red Riding Hood   Big Bad Wolf
X   X

Little Red Riding Hood: (happily) Hi, my name's Little Red Riding Hood and I'm the star of this story. First of all, let me explain something to you. You'll probably notice that the narrator is sitting way back there [points]. We thought about it for a long time and decided that a narrator really wasn't necessary for this story. It's not that we don't like narrators—they're actually pretty nice—it's just that we felt like giving the narrator a break in this story and doing it ourselves.

So, anyway, this is the story of how I listen real carefully to my grandmother before I go to visit her on the other side of the forest. It's also about a meaningful conversation I have with the Big Bad Wolf—the same guy who used to harass little girls and break into old people's homes. But this time around he's a whole new individual! Just watch.

Little Red Riding Hood: (on the telephone) That's right Granny. I'll be real careful when I come to visit you. I'll look both ways when I cross the street, I won't talk to any strange creatures along the way, and I'll make sure I leave my house in plenty of time to arrive at your house before dark. Oh, and yes, I'll be sure to carry a can of mace with me, too. Bye, bye, Granny. I'll see you soon.

Narrator: (to audience) You know, I was just thinking. This story just isn't going to work out like it should if there's no narrator. So, if it's all right with you guys, I think I'll just jump in here and see if I can help this story along.

By now you know that Red Riding Hood is off on her visit to Granny's house. And you also probably know that she's going to meet the Big Bad Wolf along the way. So let's all get back into this story and see how Red Riding Hood handles herself in the forest.

Red Riding Hood: (singing to the tune of "It's a Beautiful Day in the Neighborhood" [the theme song from "Mr. Rogers' Neighborhood"]) It's a beautiful day for a forest walk, a beautiful day for a forest, we should watch out, we should watch out, we should watch out for strangers.

Big Bad Wolf: Hey, little girl, what are you doing?

Red Riding Hood: Obviously you're not too bright, wolfman. You must be familiar with this story by now. Can't you see that I'm on my way to Granny's house?

Big Bad Wolf: Oh, yeah, right! I guess I kinda forgot. You know it's been such a long time since I've been in this story.

Red Riding Hood: So anyway, fur face, what have you been up to lately?

Red Riding Hood: (to audience) Now look, don't be too surprised at my attitude toward this guy. He's just a wolf, not your usual story creature with long teeth and blood dripping down his face. It's not like this guy is scary or anything. He's just a wolf. A big dumb wolf. Certainly nothing to get excited about.

Big Bad Wolf: (to Red Riding Hood) Well, you see, I've been spending time with my brother lately trying to get him to a doctor. You probably met him in another story . . . he's the one with asthma. Yeah, whenever he gets around straw or sticks or even bricks he always feels like he's got to huff and puff. It's really cutting down on his social life and certainly making the local police quite suspicious of his actions. I'm trying to get him some allergy tests, but so far I haven't been too successful.

Red Riding Hood: Well, the next time you see your brother, please give him my best. I think that with a little medical help he might be able to control his heavy breathing and begin to assume a more normal lifestyle—like killing defenseless sheep and stuff like that.

Big Bad Wolf: Yeah, thanks, I'll tell him you said "Hi." By the way, what have you got in your basket there?

Red Riding Hood: Oh, just a couple of new CDs for my Granny, a few MTV videos, and some chocolate chip cookies. You know how lonely it can get out there in the middle of the forest. So I thought I'd bring along some entertainment to help her pass the time away. Say, by the way, how would you like to do me a favor?

Big Bad Wolf: Name it.

Red Riding Hood: Well, as you know, Granny is awfully lonely, she doesn't get many visitors—you know what a bad reputation this forest has. Would you mind dropping in on her every once in a while? Nothing special, just a friendly visit. Of course, there can't be any funny stuff like in the last story—no putting on her pajamas or eating her up. Those things really bother her.

Big Bad Wolf: No problem. I'd love to drop in and chat. It gets pretty lonely in the forest for us animals, too. After all, all I usually get to do is eat a few rabbits, growl a little, a sleep for most of the day. I'd love to be able to visit Granny every so often. She's good company.

Red Riding Hood: Then it's done. I guess I'd better be on my way, now. Granny will be expecting me. And since you're not going to eat my Granny or me in this story, I don't have to worry about you any more. But maybe I'll see you the next time I'm through these woods.

Big Bad Wolf: Yeah, take care. Hope to see you soon!

Narrator: Unbelievable. I guess the Big Bad Wolf has finally turned over a new leaf. From now on, it looks like he's going to be a productive member of society and an outstanding citizen of the forest. It may even change the outcome of other fairy tales, too. I'll call the three little pigs next week and let you know what I find out.

From *Frantic Frogs and Other Frankly Fractured Folktales for Readers Theatre* by Anthony D. Fredericks (Englewood, CO: Teacher Ideas Press, 1993), pp. 44–46. Used by permission of the author.

Low Fourth Grade

Skinnybones

by Barbara Park
New York: Knopf, 1982
Level: 4B

Summary: Alex "Skinnybones" Frankovitch likes to talk. He also likes to think he's pretty smart, and he's the world's champion at wisecracking. These indelible traits make "Skinnybones" a riotous character that readers will come back to again and again. In this adventure in a popular series of chapter books, Skinnybones brags his way into a battle of skills with T. J. Stoner, a legend in Little League. It looks like Alex has gotten himself into more trouble than ever. Students will be rolling in the aisles as they enjoy the antics of this somewhat lovable character.

Setting the Stage

Invite students to discuss what they know about baseball—how it's played, how runs are scored, how many players, etc. You may wish to record some of this information on a nearby chalkboard or a large sheet of newsprint.

Before Reading

Involve students in a Directed Reading Thinking Activity (see page 121). Begin by inviting them to look at the title of the book and the illustration on the cover. Ask: "What do you think this book will be about?" Encourage students to make predictions and to elaborate on the reasons for making selected predictions ("Why do you think so?"). Invite students to read to the end of Chapter Two.

During Reading

After students have read to the end of Chapter Two, ask them the following questions:

• What do you think will happen next?
• Why do you think so?
• How can you prove it?

After sufficient time for discussion, ask students to read to the end of Chapter Five. Repeat the three questions from above. Some of the predictions will be refined, some will be eliminated, and new ones will be formulated. Ask students "How do you know?" to encourage clarification or verification. Repeat this process for the end of Chapters Seven and Ten. Invite students to complete the book (you may wish to spread the reading of the book over a three- to four-day period).

After Reading

Invite students to discuss the process of making predictions. How did their perceptions of Skinnybones or the plot of the story change as they read? Did the act of making predictions stimulate them to read more of the story? What predictions were "close" and what predictions were "way off the mark"? help students understand that the act of making predictions is something all accomplished readers do.

Literature Extensions

Invite students to select one or more of the following:

1. Students will definitely want to read other books in the "Skinnybones" series. Invite them to select books from the school or public library to read. Students may wish to present oral reviews of selected books for other members of the class.

2. Invite students to re-create one of the scenes in the book and develop it into a skit. They can present the skit to another class or group of students.

3. Invite students to make a list of the personality traits of "Skinnybones." Ask one student to lay down on a large sheet of newsprint. Use a crayon to draw that person's body outline on the paper. Cut out the body outline and post it on a wall of the classroom. Invite students to pretend that the outline is that of Alex. Encourage them to write the personality characteristics of Alex inside the body outline.

4. Invite students to create an oversized group mural of a significant event or memorable occurrence from the story. Students may wish to cut photos or illustrations from old magazines or develop their own original drawings for posting on the mural.

5. If possible, invite a player from the local high school baseball team to talk with your students about some of the finer points of the game (such as how to field a ground ball, how to swing a bat, or how to tag a base runner). Students may wish to develop a set of questions for the visitor based upon specific events in the book.

Summary: Daniel and his mother look out of their window at the smoky night below. There are looters on the street, fires in the distance, and chaos everywhere. Daniel clutches his cat; later, when they're forced to leave their apartment building, the cat can't be found. This is a story, not just about lost cats, but rather about how people are brought together as a result of terrible events before them. This book won the Caldecott Medal in 1995 for its stunning illustrative work by David Diaz.

Smoky Night

by Eve Bunting
San Diego: Harcourt Brace, 1994
Level: 4B

Setting the Stage

Involve students in a discussion of what they do when they are angry and frustrated. Are there other alternatives to the behaviors they describe? Explain that this book is about the way some adults behave when they too are angry and frustrated.

Before Reading

Involve students in a Story Impressions activity (see page 119). Provide each student with a listing of some of the significant events in the story. Type this list of events down the left-hand side of a sheet of paper and duplicate it for all students in a guided reading group. Invite them to read the list and then develop their own impression of the story. Students can work individually or in pairs to create and develop an appropriate story. Plan time for students to share their Story Impressions with each other.

The following story events can be used for this activity:

people rioting
stealing TVs
flicker of flames
Mrs. Kim's market
smell of smoke
missing cat
at the shelter
firefighter holding cats
drinking milk

During Reading

Invite students to read the story on their own. Encourage them to look for some of the events presented in the "Before Reading" stage.

After Reading

Have students review the story they created prior to reading the book. What differences do they note between their initial impressions and the actual content of the story? Plan time to discuss those differences. You may wish to have students rewrite their stories in keeping with the plot of the book.

Literature Extensions

Invite students to select one or more of the following:

1. Have students write a sequel to the story. What will happen between Daniel's mother and Mrs. Kim? What will happen between the two cats? How will the neighborhood look? How will the neighborhood be fixed up? Plan sufficient time for students to share their endings with each other.

2. Eve Bunting is one of this country's most well-respected and well-known children's authors. Students may wish to obtain information about this popular author through the following website:

http://www.friend.ly.net/scoop/biographies/ buntingeve/index.html

Invite students to assemble a biographical sketch of Eve Bunting to contribute to the school library.

3. Discuss different kinds of families with the group. This book portrays a single-parent family. In a comfortable atmosphere, invite students to share the different types of families of which they are a part. Discuss the varieties of families there are. Students may wish to create a large class collage of the various family types represented in the guided reading group or classroom. This can be posted on a classroom bulletin board.

4. Discuss with students different ways, techniques, and methods of resolving conflicts. Why do people get upset with each other in the first place? How can they resolve their differences without resorting to arguing, fighting, or rioting? You may wish to invite the school counselor into your classroom to share some conflict resolution techniques with the group or class. Students may want to propose some resolution strategies that could have been used to prevent the riots depicted in the book.

5. If possible, invite a firefighter to discuss safety precautions to help prevent accidental fires and measures families can take in the event of fire.

6. Author Eve Bunting dedicated the book to the peacekeepers. Discuss the question, "Who are the peacekeepers?" Can each student be a peacekeeper? How? Invite students to create a bulletin board that reflects and honors the peacekeepers of the world.

High Fourth Grade

The Giver

by Lois Lowry
New York: Bantam Doubleday, 1993
Level: 4C

Summary: Everything in Jonas's world is perfect: there is no hunger, pain, or war. But in Jonas's world, there are also no choices. Everyone is assigned a specific job when they are 12 years old; Jonas is given the honor of being selected to become the "Receiver of Memories" and begins training with the Giver. As the memories of the past fill Jonas with new feelings, including love and pain, he is compelled to discover his own truths and reality.

Setting the Stage

Discuss the title and its possible meanings. Who might "The Giver" be and what might his role involve? Invite students to study the illustrations on the cover and make interpretations based on the pictures, colors used, and layout.

Before Reading

Provide students with a copy of a sample Plot Graph (if you wish, copy and duplicate the one in this book on page 175). Help students understand how a good book begins with several events, builds to a climactic point, and then reaches a conclusion. Invite students to be aware of the events in this book and how they might be added to a Plot Graph done upon completion of the book.

During Reading

Invite students to read the book on their own (Note: This is an extended book that includes 23 long chapters. It will be necessary to extend the reading over a period of several days.) This is also a challenging read for fourth-grade readers due to some of the vocabulary. It will be necessary to provide assistance to individual students on an "as needed" basis.

After Reading

Upon completion of the book, have students discuss the four or five most significant events—in other words, what events would they wish to list along the bottom of a Plot Graph? Invite students to reach some decisions and create a group Plot Graph using their selected events. Record numbers along the left side of the graph as in the example on page 175 of this resource book. Now, encourage students to make appropriate Xs on the graph and to connect those Xs with straight lines. Point out to students how the lines indicate the development of the story and its sequence of significant events. Mention to students that all good books have approximately the same design—building events, a climax, and concluding events.

Literature Extensions

Invite students to select one or more of the following:

1. After students have read Chapters One through Four, invite them to make a list of things that seem unusual and that suggest that Jonas's society is far different from ours. For each item listed, encourage students to consider the implications and make predictions as to what each actually implies.

2. Invite students to create their own utopian society. To prepare, they need to determine what problems in our current society will be eliminated in their own and how this will be accomplished. Encourage them to create a visual "floor plan" to illustrate the society.

3. Ask students to write a sequel to the story. What happens next to Jonas and Gabriel as they follow the music? Invite students to tape their stories or write them in book form and illustrate.

4. One of the most important themes of *The Giver* deals with the importance of memory. Invite students to select one of their most important memories that involves a member (or members) of their family. Ask them to summarize the memory, illustrate it, and send it with a card to the family members most responsible for this special time and thank them for the memory.

5. Select various issues reflected in the book and invite pairs of students to debate each, being sure to cite specific references from the book. Issues can include:

- Does the government have the right to make laws to protect people from learning about things that might hurt them?

- Should free choice be limited? Who should set these limits and how?

- Is "sameness" a valid way of life if it prevents prejudice and discrimination?

- Is there any possible way to create a utopian way of life?

- Is "release" humane or inhumane?

Summary: Stanley Yelnats is sent to Camp Green Lake as a juvenile offender in this Newbery Medal book. Unfortunately there is no lake, but there are lots of wide-open spaces and lots of work. Each of the inmates must dig a hole—a hole five feet by five feet—every single day. The warden says that this work will build character and make the boys better citizens, but Stanley suspects that something else is up as he plunges into a mystery that will keep the pages turning and the laughter flowing. Students won't be able to put this chapter book down; it is fantastic addition to any classroom library.

Holes

by Louis Sachar
New York: Farrar, Straus and Giroux, 1998
Level: 4C

Setting the Stage	Ask students to discuss a time in their lives in which they were blamed for something they didn't do. Provide opportunities for students to share those events as well as their feelings about the events. Plan time to discuss ways to handle situations such as these.
Before Reading	Provide students in a guided reading group with a copy of Literature Log I (see page 177). Inform them that they will be completing this log upon conclusion of the book. Take a few minutes to go over the elements of the Log with group members.
During Reading	Invite students to read several chapters each day. (*Note*: The book has 50 short chapters.) The book should be read silently while you assist students on an individual basis with difficult vocabulary and concepts.
After Reading	Upon completion of the book, ask students to fill in the appropriate information on the Literature Log. Students may wish to complete these on an individual basis or in pairs. Plan time afterward for students to share their Logs. What similarities are there among Logs? What differences are there?

Literature Extensions

Invite students to select one or more of the following:

1. As they are reading *Holes,* invite students to keep a simulated journal, one in which they write as if they are one of the main characters in the book. Allow time for students to discuss their journal entries as well as their feelings and insights.

2. Involve students in a mock trial in which they try Stanley for the theft of the sneakers.

3. Stanley's father was involved in finding ways to recycle sneakers. Ask group members to brainstorm a list of ways that sneakers can be recycled. From this list, ask them to select one and create a plan to recycle sneakers.

4. *Holes* relates the legend of Kissin' Kate Barlow. Either individually, or in pairs, invite students to create another version to explain Kate Barlow's metamorphosis from upstanding citizen to outlaw.

5. At the end of the book, the author writes that many changes took place in the $1\frac{1}{2}$ years after Stanley and Hector left Camp Green Lake. He encourages the reader to "fill in the holes." On a large sheet of construction paper, draw at least five holes. For each hole, ask students to predict one event they believe may have happened during this time period to the main characters and/or their families.

6. Invite students to research life in a local juvenile detention center. What is life typically like for the juveniles sent there? How does the center differ from Camp Green Lake?

Hurricanes: Earth's Mightiest Storms

by Patricia Lauber
New York: Scholastic Press, 1996
Level: 4D

Summary: This is a masterful work that examines and effectively describes the power, intensity, and history of hurricanes. The author, who has done her homework thoroughly, begins by describing a little-known hurricane that struck the East Coast in 1938. As she tracks the hurricane, readers learn how hurricanes form, how they travel, and the incredible destruction they create across the landscape. Hurricane formation, how they are named, measuring devices, the science of tracking hurricanes, and the overwhelming destruction they cause are all presented via compelling text. The book ends with an eye to the future and the environmental implications of hurricanes in the years to come.

Setting the Stage

Before passing out copies of the book to the members of a guided reading group, read page 7 and page 8 (down the first column through the fifth paragraph, which ends, ". . . no warnings were sent ahead"). Afterward, invite students to make some predictions about this particular storm. What will happen? What kind of damage will occur? Take a few minutes to discuss and share all predictions.

Before Reading

Invite students to participate in a K-W-L activity (see page 105). Ask students to talk about what they already know about hurricanes. Write this information in the K section of a K-W-L chart. Encourage students to categorize the information they have volunteered. Students may wish to create a semantic web of this data. Invite students to make predictions about the types of information the book will contain. Write these predictions on a chalkboard or large sheet of newsprint. Ask students to generate their own questions about the book. These can be discussed and recorded in the W—What we want to find out—section of the chart.

During Reading

Invite students to read the book and record any answers to their questions. Students may wish to do this individually or in pairs.

After Reading

Upon completion of the book, provide students with an opportunity to discuss the information learned and how that data relates to their prior knowledge. Talk about questions posed for which no information was found in the book. Help students discover other sources for satisfying their inquiries.

Literature Extensions

Invite students to select one or more of the following:

1. Have students imagine that they are in a hurricane-prone area. What types of precautions should they take if a hurricane approaches? What types of precautions are appropriate at other times of the year? How can families better prepare themselves for future hurricanes? Invite students to assemble a hurricane safety book that could be distributed through a local chapter of the American Red Cross or other disaster relief agency.

2. The following website—http://www.sun-sentinel.com/storm/history/— presents a time line of Atlantic Ocean hurricanes from the time of Christopher Columbus to the present. Invite students to log on to the site and select the "Top Ten" hurricanes of all time. Encourage students to create their own time line of these "Top Ten." Post the time line on a wall of the classroom.

3. The book briefly mentions how hurricanes are named. Tell students to imagine that they are being put in charge of naming the hurricanes for the forthcoming hurricane season. What names (in alphabetical order) would they give to the hurricanes? Why are those names appropriate? Inform students that the names used are random and alternate between female and male names. Ask students to consider whether the names should have some sort of historical or personal significance.

4. On page 27 of the book, the author describes the various names given to these storms around the world (such as hurricanes, cyclones, typhoons, and willy-willies). Invite students to create a poster or mural that describes each of these storms, where they are located, and how they got their names. This can be posted on a wall of the classroom or in the school library.

A River Ran Wild

by Lynne Cherry
San Diego: Harcourt Brace, 1992
Level: 4C

Summary: A beautifully illustrated book, this story concerns the "life history" of the Nashua River in New England. The stories of the people who lived along its banks, their customs, traditions, and culture and how those were shaped by the forces and resources of the river are powerfully told. The author then tells how the people polluted their river with toxins and how several residents helped return the river to its original state.

Setting the Stage

Provide a copy of the book to each student in a guided reading group. Invite students to "thumb" through the book and closely observe the illustrations arranged around the perimeter of the pages on the left side of each spread. What do they notice about those illustrations? How does each set of illustrations change as the book progresses? How might the illustrations be related to the story?

Before Reading

Ask students to define the word *pollution*. Invite them to describe different forms of pollution. Where does pollution occur? Who is responsible for pollution? What are the long-term effects of a polluted environment? Don't provide any answers—just encourage students to discuss the implications.

During Reading

Ask students to read the entire book to themselves while noting how, over time, the Nashua River becomes polluted. Assist individual students with difficult vocabulary or concepts.

After Reading

Type up the page in the book (pages are not numbered) that begins with "The paper mills continued to pollute. . . ." Using the Answer First! Format (see page 157), type up the answers to five questions at the bottom of the sheet. Provide copies of the sheet to the entire group. Invite group members to generate the five questions for the answers you provided. Include several higher-level thinking answers on the sheet.

Literature Extensions

Invite students to select one or more of the following:

1. Ask students to contact various community agencies and county groups on environmental preservation efforts in your local area. What is being done by local groups, organizations, and governmental bodies to preserve and protect the local environment?

2. Encourage students to establish a litter patrol for your school. They may wish to establish a recruiting station to solicit volunteers for their teams, place posters in and around the school, establish regular patrols throughout the school grounds, and create a flyer or newsletter about the cleanup to be sent to administrators.

3. The following websites offer students loads of fascinating information about the environment and about their roles in protecting and preserving it:

http://tqjunior.advanced.org/3715

http://eelink.net/sitemap.html

http://takeaction.worldwildlife.org

4. Invite students to question neighbors in their community about how they work to preserve and protect the plants and animals in the local area. Have students gather their findings into various charts and graphs to be displayed in the classroom.

Sideways Stories from Wayside School

by Louis Sachar
New York: Avon Books, 1978
Level: 4D

Summary: Wayside school is strange—really strange! First of all, it was supposed to be built with 30 classrooms all next to each other in a row. Instead, the builder (who said he was sorry) built the classrooms one on top of the other, 30 stories high. That's probably why all sorts of weird and crazy things happen at Wayside School, especially on the 30th floor. Here, students will meet Mrs. Gorf, the meanest teacher of all; Joe who has the strangest way of adding numbers; and a host of other characters who will keep students in stitches and the pages turning with wild abandon. Be ready for snickers, giggles, and guffaws aplenty.

Setting the Stage

Read the Introduction on page 9 of the book out loud to the students. Show them the illustration on the cover. Invite students to make some predictions about Wayside School and some of the characters who might appear in the story.

Before Reading

Inform students that you will involve them in a reading strategy known as the Reflective Sharing Technique (see page 115). In the middle of a chalkboard, write the word *school*. For approximately three to five minutes, invite students to brainstorm as many ideas, concepts, or items that can be included within that topic. Ask each student to select one of the brainstormed items from the list on the board. Invite each student to write about her or his selected item for about five minutes. Arrange the students into groups of four and assign each person a role (Person 1: Reader; Person 2: Summarizer; Person 3: Teller; Person 4: Like to know). Invite students to repeat the process of sharing until they have gone through all four rounds.

During Reading

Have students read the book independently. You may wish to have students read three to four chapters each day over a period of several days (there are 30 chapters in the book).

After Reading

After students have finished the book, invite them to discuss some of their favorite characters. Which ones were similar to people that they know? Which ones were similar to classmates? Which ones were similar to them? Engage students in a conversation about how Wayside School is similar to or different from their school. Is Wayside School a place you would like to attend? Are the students in the book people you would like to have as classmates?

Literature Extensions

Invite students to select one or more of the following:

1. Encourage students to imagine that they must create a yearbook for the students at Wayside School. Fasten 30 sheets of paper together into a folder or binder. Invite each student to select several sheets and on each one draw an illustration of one of the characters along with any accompanying information. This would be an appropriate group activity upon completion of the book.

2. Students will certainly be interested in reading other books about Wayside School, including *Wayside School Is Falling Down* and *Wayside School Gets a Little Stranger.*

3. Talk with students about some of the qualities of good teachers. What should good teachers do? How should they act toward their students? How should they teach? Invite students to assemble their data in the form of a brochure or leaflet that can be shared with the principal, superintendent, or school board.

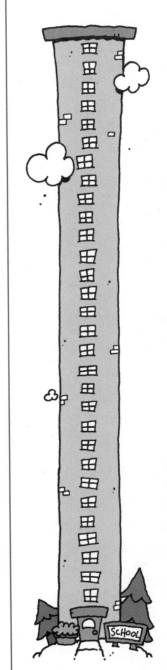

4. Invite students to write a 31st story for the book. Invite them to imagine that one more student has transferred into Wayside School. What characteristics or features will that character have? What kind of escapades will that character get into?

5. Invite students to write an imaginary letter to Louis Sachar, the author of the book. Students may wish to tell him how much they liked the book, how much the characters are like people they know, how much Wayside School is like their school, or even about a brand new story for a forthcoming books about Wayside School that the author is writing.

6. Invite students to make a "Wanted" poster for one of the students in Wayside School. What kind of information should be included on the poster? Place the finished poster on a special bulletin board in the classroom. Have students create other posters for other characters.

7. Have students look through several old magazines and cut out pictures of children they would like to have in their classroom. Encourage students to paste these pictures on a large sheet of paper. Talk about why the selected children would be welcome in their classroom.

Summary: David Alspeth sets sail on an incredible voyage of self-discovery and survival in this gripping tale of loneliness, courage, and determination. Fulfilling his uncle's last wish, David sails out into the ocean in the *Frog,* but a sudden and savage storm slams into his sailboat and casts David into the adventure of his life. With no radio, no water, and no wind, David must face the unknown and figure out a way to survive by himself. This is a classic tale from an award-winning author that is guaranteed to have students coming back for more.

The Voyage of the Frog

by Gary Paulsen
New York: Dell, 1989
Level: 4C

Setting the Stage

Share the cover of the book with a guided reading group. Invite students to make some predictions about the story based entirely on the cover. What will this book be about? What are some events that might happen? What is the *Frog*? How will the story end?

Before Reading

Inform students that you will be leading them through a guided reading strategy known as the No Book DR-TA (see page 116). First, invite students in a group to list everything they can think of that might pertain to sailing. Students may wish to brainstorm items individually or in pairs. The entire group maintains a master list. Ask students to group all the items on the list into categories (it may be necessary for you to model the categorizing behavior for students initially). Ask students to assign a name for each category as though they were a table of contents for a book. Invite each student to write a brief "book" about the topic of sailing using the categories as chapter titles. Encourage students to write as much about each topic as they can, summarizing what each section is about. If students get stuck, they are allowed to make up what they don't know. Keep the finished books "on file."

During Reading

Provide each student with a copy of the book and invite him or her to read it silently. (*Note:* The book has 18 chapters and the reading can be spread out over several days.) Invite students to note some of the skills and processes involved in sailing as they read.

After Reading

Have students return to their No Book DR-TA stories. What new information from the book can they add to their stories? Plan some time for students to select and include appropriate data in addition to sharing ideas in a mutually supportive environment.

Literature Extensions

Invite students to select one or more of the following:

1. The story ends with David still out on the ocean. Invite students to write a sequel to the book. What happens to David and the *Frog*? What does he do when he gets back home?

2. Invite students to assemble items they would take with them if they were to set out on a long-distance voyage on the ocean. What essential foods (nonperishable) would they take? What types of clothing? What equipment or supplies? Remind students that they have limited space on their boat and may be on the water for a long time.

3. Have students share stories about journeys, trips, or vacations they have taken. What makes those trips so memorable? Why do people travel? What is the fascination of a trip? Students may wish to assemble their memories into a travel notebook for display in the classroom.

4. Invite a sailor (professional or recreational) to your classroom to describe some of the things she or he must do when preparing for a voyage. How is the trip planned? What precautions are taken? What supplies or equipment are taken? Students may wish to compare the visitor's preparations with those of David. What are the similarities or differences?

5. Here's an activity that will give students an opportunity to create and observe simulated waves:

Materials

a clear empty two-liter soda bottle
  (with screw-on top)
salad oil
water
blue food coloring

Directions

a. Fill an empty two-liter soda bottle $1/3$ of the way with salad oil.

b. Fill the rest of the bottle (all the way to the brim) with water dyed with a few drops of food coloring.

c. Put the top on securely and lay the bottle on its side. Now, slowly and gently tip the bottle back and forth.

The oil in the bottle will roll and move just like the waves in the ocean. Students will have created a miniature ocean in a bottle. Waves are energy that moves through water. It is not the water that moves, but rather the energy in the water that causes waves to occur. Ocean waves are generated by the gravitational pull of the moon on Earth's surface, the geological formation of the ocean floor, and the movement of wind across the surface of the water. Students can artificially create waves in a soda bottle and observe wave action that is quite similar to that which occurs throughout the oceans of the world.

Low Fifth Grade

Bridge to Terabithia

by Katherine Paterson
New York: Harper & Row, 1989
Level: 5B

Summary: Jess and Leslie become friends and establish a secret meeting place deep in the woods, where they have created an imaginary kingdom called Terabithia. Their friendship comes to an end when Leslie falls into the swollen stream that must be crossed to reach Terabithia. Jess builds a bridge across the stream as a lasting token of their friendship. This book, which won the Newbery Medal in 1978, is a testament to the power of friendship and the trials and tribulations of growing up. It will spark discussion among students as few books can. It is a book to be savored and enjoyed for many years.

Setting the Stage

Invite students to discuss the qualities they look for in a friend. What is a friend? What do friends do for each other? What must be done to maintain a friendship?

Before Reading

Provide each student with one of the following: a Story Frame, a Plot Frame, or a Character Analysis Frame (see page 160). Take a few minutes to discuss each frame and the information that will need to be written in the appropriate spaces. Indicate to students that these frames will help them organize their thoughts about a story.

During Reading

Invite students to read the book silently to themselves (*Note:* The book has 13 chapters and will take several days to read.) As necessary, assist individual students with difficult vocabulary or complicated concepts. Encourage students to visualize some of the settings and events of the story as they are reading. This will aid them in completing their frames.

After Reading

Upon finishing the book, ask each student to complete her or his individual frame. Plan sufficient time for students to share and discuss their respective frames. How were their perceptions similar? How were they different?

Literature Extensions

Invite students to select one or more of the following:

1. Using butcher paper or a large sheet of newsprint, have each student make a life-sized cutout of her or his best friend. Students can draw or color the physical features of the friend. Ask each student to cut a "door" into the chest area to view a list of inner qualities that make the friend special. (The qualities can be written on a separate piece of paper, cut slightly larger than the door, and glued or taped behind the door.) Plan opportunities for students to discuss the qualities that make their friends so special.

2. This book addresses a topic not often found in children's literature: death. Plan opportunities for students to read other books about death including one or more of the following:

Death Is Natural by Laurence Pringle
The Kid's Book About Death and Dying by Eric Rofes
Learning to Say Goodbye by Eda LeShan
The Tenth Good Thing About Barney by Judith Viorst
When People Die by Joanne E. Bernstein

3. After Leslie's death, Jess needed time to learn how to cope with his feelings. Several characters in the story helped him with this process. Invite students to identify these characters and discuss how they helped Jess. The ideas can be written on "helping hands"—hand-shaped cutouts. For example, Jess's father listened to his fears and held him close; Mrs. Myers shared her feelings about her husband's death; and Bill gave Jess a puppy for which to care.

4. Leslie and Jess pretend that they are rulers of a magic kingdom. Have each student create a story about a kingdom she or he would like to rule.

5. Ask students to discuss some of the reasons why Jess decided to build a bridge across the stream. What was the symbolism in this event? Why did the author decide to include this event in the story?

Summary: Filled with awe-inspiring details, this book gives readers incredible facts and information about the world's largest land animal. The narrator (a native of Kenya) offers readers insights into this often misunderstood animal. The book provides a wonderful bridge between social studies and science.

Elephants for Kids

by Anthony D. Fredericks
Minnetonka, MN: NorthWord Press, 1999
Level: 5A

Setting the Stage

Distribute copies of the book to each student in a guided reading group. Invite students to look at the cover of the book and describe what they see. How does that photograph compare with the knowledge they already have about elephants?

Before Reading

Prepare an Anticipation Guide for the book (see page 106). Provide each student with a photocopied sheet that has the following statements typed on it:

a. Elephants live in Africa.

b. All elephants have tusks.

c. Elephants are the world's largest land animals.

d. Elephants drink lots of water.

e. Elephants are an endangered species.

f. Elephants always live in large herds.

Invite students to agree or disagree with each of the statements.

During Reading

Students can read the entire book in one sitting. Invite students to look for confirmation of the Anticipation Guide statements as they are reading. Assist individual students with difficult vocabulary during the silent reading process.

After Reading

After students have completed the book, ask them to re-read the Anticipation Guide statements and decide which ones are correct and which ones are incorrect. Plan time for students to confirm or verify their decisions by re-reading appropriate passages. Ask students to talk about changes they made in their pre-reading knowledge and their post-reading knowledge.

Literature Extensions

Invite students to select one or more of the following:

1. Have students present a mini-lesson to another class on elephants. The lesson can be presented in person or via a video tape.

2. Invite a zoologist or biologist from a local college to visit your classroom and share information related to elephants. Have group members prepare questions beforehand to be sent to the guest speaker.

3. Have children write to the National Wildlife Federation (8925 Leesburg Pike, Vienna, VA 22184) and ask for information on endangered species. The NWF's website (http://www.nwf.org) is an excellent resource for information on endangered species.

4. Students may wish to log on to a fascinating website on the country of Kenya. This site (http://www.supersurf.com/kenya/) was created by a 12-year-old boy in Phoenix, Arizona.

5. Students may enjoy creating a book of elephant facts. After they have read this book, invite them to obtain several books and resources from the school or public library on elephants and their habits to use as additional reference tools.

Literature Extensions

Invite students to select one or more of the following:

1. Encourage students to read other books by Gary Paulsen. They may enjoy reading the sequel to *Hatchet: The River* (New York: Dell, 1991). Afterward, students may wish to compare the two books via a Venn Diagram.

2. Invite students to check with the local Red Cross, the regional FEMA agency, or an environmental group on survival skills needed for travel in the wilderness. Students may be able to obtain information via library books or Internet resources. Invite pairs of students to gather their information into a survival guide for students. What information would be most useful? Can they design an informational brochure that would have been useful for Brian?

3. Invite each student in a guided reading group to create an alternate ending for the story. What might have happened if the rescue plane had not seen Brian? Ask each student to write her or his own ending and then share it with the group.

4. Have each student write an imaginary letter to Brian. What would they like to say to him after his ordeal? What else about his adventure would they like to know? How is Brian dealing physically and emotionally after this incident?

5. Invite someone from a local hiking or orienteering club (check the local phone book) to visit the class and discuss some of the physical skills necessary for surviving in the wilderness. Students may wish to share specific events from the story with the visitor for comments or suggestions on whether Brian did the proper thing.

6. Obtain one or more topological maps of your state from the public library or geography department of a local college. Ask students to observe the different geographical features. Is there any area of your state that would be similar to the topography or terrain where Brian was?

Jeremy Thatcher, Dragon Hatcher

by Bruce Coville
New York: Simon & Schuster, 1991
Level: 5D

Summary: Jeremy purchases a dragon—not just any dragon, but one that gets him into all kinds of unimaginable trouble with his friends and family. This is a riotous tale by a master storyteller that will keep young readers asking for more.

Setting the Stage

Ask students the following question: If you could own any kind of imaginary pet, what would it be? Invite students to think about their responses for a few minutes. They don't need to verbalize their answers.

Before Reading

Provide each student with a copy of the book. Take a few moments to share each of the illustrations in the book with the group. Invite students to make some predictions about the content of the book. Tell students that while they are reading this book, you would like for them to use some "student-posed" metacognitive questions (see page 126). They may wish to jot down a few questions and the responses while they are reading.

During Reading

Each day students will read two or three of the chapters silently. Take a few moments at the beginning of each day to discuss the metacognitive questions students asked themselves during the previous day's reading. Talk about some of the ways in which they answered their own questions.

After Reading

Make a master list of all the metacognitive questions students asked during the reading of the book. Review those questions for the group as well as some of the ways in which individual group members arrived at their individual answers. What were some strategies or techniques individuals used to help them understand and appreciate the story?

Literature Extensions

Invite students to select one or more of the following:

1. At the end of the story, the dragon, Tiamat, enters a new world. Have students write a letter to Tiamat in her new world. They may wish to inquire about where she lives, her friends, and whether she thinks about Jeremy. Ask students to share their letters with each other.

2. Jeremy got the name for his dragon from a list of great dragons he had made at the library. Invite students to create their own list of dragon names. Which one would they choose if they were naming a dragon?

3. Invite students to create a manual on the care and feeding of dragons. What kinds of information should they include in the manual? Who would be the audience for the manual—kids or adults? How should they organize the manual? Have students look at pet care books (available in pet stores) for examples.

4. Encourage students to create an original dragon dictionary. Have them collect dragon-related words from various books and resources and compile those words into a dictionary (cut into the shape of a dragon).

5. Provide students with empty shoeboxes, various pieces of colored construction paper, glues, scissors, and other art materials. Ask students (individually or in pairs) to design dioramas of selected scenes from the book.

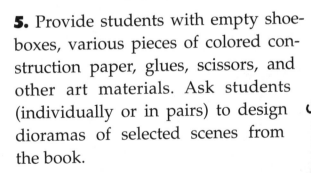

Missing May

by Cynthia Rylant
New York: Dell, 1993
Level: 5D

Summary: This compelling book by an award-winning author is one of discovery and revelation. It is the story of Summer, who has lived with her aunt and uncle since she was six years old. Now her aunt has died and Summer is afraid of what will happen to Uncle Ob. With the companionship of a strange boy from school, Summer and Uncle Ob set off on a most unusual journey to search for some sign from Aunt May. All three are looking for a way to ease their pain and sorrow and discover a strength none of them knew they had before. This is a touching tale by a masterful storyteller that will spark much discussion in the classroom. This book won the Newbery Medal in 1993.

Setting the Stage

Pass out a copy of the book to each student. Invite students to look at the cover illustration and the title. What can they infer from these two items? Does the illustration give any information about the content of the story? Why is the book titled *Missing May?* Plan a few moments to discuss students' perceptions.

Before Reading

Engage students in using a Possible Sentences strategy (see page 118). Provide students in a guided reading group with a list of words from the book such as these:

died	unexpected	ghost	strange
curious	weird	afterlife	funeral
vision	journey	discovery	suitcase

Invite each student to select two words from the list and use them in an original sentence. After each student has created a sentence, plan time to discuss the sentences and how they might relate to the plot of the story.

During Reading

The book is written in two parts. Invite students to read Part One on one day and Part Two on the following day. Remind students to watch for the words or concepts they shared as part of the "Before Reading" time.

After Reading

Have students re-visit their Possible Sentences. What changes do they need to make in those sentences? Can they write some new sentences using those words? How did their original ideas about the story change by the end of the story? What would be some appropriate sentences to share with other members of the class who have not read the book?

Literature Extensions

Ask students to select one or more of the following:

1. Invite students to imagine that each of them was traveling with Summer, Uncle Ob, and Cletis. Have students keep an imaginary diary of their thoughts, ideas, and perceptions during the trip. Plan time for students to discuss their respective diaries.

2. Encourage students to read other books by Cynthia Rylant. They may wish to obtain copies of *A Blue-Eyed Daisy*, *A Kindness*, *A Couple of Kooks and Other Stories About Love*, and/or *A Fine White Dust*.

3. Cynthia Rylant grew up in West Virginia and that's where this story takes place. Provide students with a map of West Virginia and invite them to locate some of the places and sites mentioned in the book. Students may wish to consult library or Internet resources for additional information about West Virginia.

4. Based upon the information in the book, invite students to create their own whirlygigs. They may wish to create a whirligig in honor of one of the three main characters in the story.

5. Invite students to write a prequel to the story. What should people know about May? What kind of person was she? What were some of the things she would have done? Plan opportunities for students to share their stories with each other.

The Rough-Face Girl

by Rafe Martin
New York: Putnam's, 1992
Level: 5C

Summary: A scarred face does not prevent the rough-face girl from seeing the beauty of Earth around her, nor does it disguise her beautiful, kind heart in this award-winning retelling of a powerful Algonquin Cinderella. This is a book to share again and again.

Setting the Stage

Provide individual copies of the book to each student. Tell students that this story is an Algonquin Indian version of the "Cinderella" story. Inform students that, according to some estimates, there are more than 300 versions of the "Cinderella" story from around the world.

Before Reading

Provide each student with a photocopied sheet of paper on which you have drawn a Venn diagram. Invite students to write the title of this book (*The Rough-Face Girl*) over one circle and the Cinderella title over the other circle. Have students, as they are reading, to list events from this book in one of the circles. Encourage students to read the book in one sitting.

During Reading

As students read, have them write story events in the appropriate circle on the Venn diagram. Assist individual students as necessary.

After Reading

After students have finished reading the story, invite them to record any events they recall from the traditional version of "Cinderella." What similarities and/or differences do they note in the two versions? Students may enjoy producing the humorous Readers Theatre adaptation of Cinderella (*The Underappreciated Fairy Godmother [Known as Roxanne to Her Friends] Gets Really Ticked Off*) duplicated on page 268. (See page 161 for more on this technique.) Invite students to produce this version and discuss any similarities and/or differences between this adaptation and the version or versions with which they are more familiar.

Literature Extensions

Invite students to select one or more of the following:

1. The stars were an important part of Native American stories and culture. Your students may enjoy investigating the role of stars and constellations through Native American Astronomy's delightful and informative website: http://indy4.fdl.cc.mn.us/~isk/stars/starmenu.html.

2. The Algonquin Indians were located primarily along the upper Ottawa River in Canada. Have students calculate the distance from their town or city to this part of North America. Hang a large world map on the wall and invite students to plot a travel route to this part of the world.

3. Invite students to create a sequel to the story that focuses on the life of the Rough-Face Girl and the Invisible Being. How did they spend their lives after they were married?

4. Students may wish to investigate specific information about the Algonquin Indians. The website at http://tqjunior.thinkquest.org/6299/algon.htm is devoted exclusively to the Algonquins, their customs, their traditions, and their lifestyle.

The Underappreciated Fairy Godmother (Known as Roxanne to Her Friends) Gets Really Ticked Off

Staging: For this presentation the narrator should be placed at a podium or lectern near the center of the staging area. Note that the audience has several parts throughout the production.

Really Beautiful Cinderella Lady
X

Really Handsome Prince Guy
X

Roxanne, the Underappreciated Fairy Godmother
X

Narrator
X

Audience

X   X   X   X   X   X   X   X

X   X   X   X   X   X   X   X

Narrator: You all remember the story about Cinderella? You know, the girl who spent her days scrubbing kitchen floors down at the local castle until the fairy godmother comes along and magically turns her into some really beautiful damsel and then magically turns a pumpkin into some luxury coach and magically turns the mice into her personal servants? And then, Cindy goes off to the ball where she meets a real hunk of a prince, loses her shoe, he finds her, has her try on the shoe, they marry, and yadda, yadda, yadda. You remember all that?

Audience: (somewhat indignantly) Yes, oh great and magnificent Narrator, we remember.

Narrator: O.K., let's not get testy here. Anyway, as I was saying, everybody in that story lives happily ever after except for one individual.

3. Invite students to talk about the roles and responsibilities of neighbors. What is a neighbor? What does a neighbor do for others in his or her community? What makes a neighborhood a neighborhood?

4. Invite students to create a community newspaper. Students may wish to create current-event articles on the local neighborhood, a series of community cartoons, a sports page, movie and play reviews and schedules, PTO meetings, and so on.

5. Invite students to write journal entries about one thing in their own neighborhoods they would like to change. Why did they select that particular item? How would they change it?

Low Sixth Grade

Cannibal Animals: Animals That Eat Their Own Kind

by Anthony D. Fredericks
New York: Watts, 1999
Level: 6A

Summary: Animals practice cannibalism to survive in an uncertain environment. This captivating and fascinating book shows how and why praying mantises, black widow spiders, lions, sharks, chimpanzees—even furry gerbils—sometimes kill and eat members of their own kind. Filled with jaw-dropping photography and a wealth of incredible information, this book will keep students talking long after they finish it and will become a valuable resource for any animal unit in science.

Setting the Stage

Invite students to share what they know about cannibalism. Where did they get their information? How accurate is their information? What uncertainties do they have about the topic?

Before Reading

Invite students to participate in a Concept Cards activity (see page 100). Print the following words on a set of 3-x-5-inch index cards and distribute them to students prior to their reading of the book:

survival	species	evolution
extinct	exoskeleton	competition
dangerous	spiders	larva
egg	guppy	salamander
Tyrannosaurus	frog	shark
oxygen	gerbil	litter
bear	chimpanzee	cannibalism
behavior	gestation	prey

During Reading

After students have arranged their cards into categories and defended the cards within each category, have them read all six chapters of the book independently. Encourage students to look for words they saw on the concept cards.

Summary: Charles Wallace and the unicorn Gaudior take a perilous journey through time to prevent the mad dictator Madog Branzillo from destroying the world. Adventures abound in this fantasy tale that will keep readers spellbound and asking questions for which there may be no real answers. The author is at her best in this addition to an amazing trilogy that is captivating as much as it is engaging. Imaginations will soar and conversations will be infused with the magical adventures here and in students' minds.

A Swiftly Tilting Planet

by Madeleine L'Engle
New York: Dell, 1986
Level: 6B

Setting the Stage

Talk with students about how they would feel if they were responsible for saving the world. What would be the first thing they would do? What special skills do the students have that could be used to save the world? What difficulties might be anticipated?

Before Reading

Provide each student with a Character Analysis sheet (see page 187). Encourage them to talk about the qualities or characteristics they most appreciate in a good story character. What makes a good character? Afterward, invite students to identify the features they would most like to have in a story character that was going to save the world from destruction. Tell them that, as they read the story, they should focus on Charles Wallace and the characteristics that make him ideally suited for saving the world.

During Reading

Provide copies of the book to students and invite them to read it silently (this book will take several days to read). Assist, as necessary, with difficult vocabulary and scientific concepts. Remind students to focus on the personality attributes of Charles throughout the book.

After Reading

Upon completion of the book, ask students to fill in their individual Character Analysis forms. Take some time to discuss the elements each student recorded on her or his sheet. Are there similarities or differences among or between the forms? How do students account for any differences? Assist students in creating a "profile" of "The Ideal Person to Save the World." Is Charles Wallace that person or should the individual have some traits or characteristics that Charles lacks?

Literature Extensions

Invite students to select one or more of the following:

1. This book is part of a trilogy of books by Madeleine L'Engle. The other two books are *A Wind in the Door* and *A Wrinkle in Time.* Invite students to read these other books in the series.

2. Although this book is a fantasy, there are some truths or scientific principles woven throughout. Plan time to discuss with students some of the scientific principles found throughout this book. Are there specific occurrences that are based on scientific facts? How much of the book is based on imagination or impossible scientific events?

3. Invite a guided reading group to create a Reader's Theatre interpretation of one of the scenes in the book. Assign speaking roles to various individuals using the dialogue in the book. Assign a narrator to read those parts not spoken by characters.

4. Talk with students about items they would want to put into a time capsule. What items should be included in a capsule that would be opened in 100 years? What items would be most representative of the current generation? What items would give people in the future a representative glimpse of life today?

5. Invite each student to select her or his favorite setting from the book. Encourage individuals to create a diorama (using a shoebox) of that particular place. Provide the necessary space for students to display their completed dioramas.